First Steps in Parenting the Child Who Hurts

Companion volume

Next Steps in Parenting the Child Who Hurts
Tykes and Teens
Caroline Archer, Adoption UK
ISBN 978 1 85302 802 1

of related interest

The Adoption Experience
Families who Give Children a Second Chance
Ann Morris, Adoption UK
ISBN 978 1 85302 783 3

Lesbian and Gay Fostering and Adoption
Extraordinary Yet Ordinary
Edited by Stephen Hicks and Janet McDermott
ISBN 978 1 85302 600 3

Adopting a Child
A Guidebook for Adoptive Parents and Their Advisors
R.A.C. Hoksbergen
ISBN 978 1 85302 415 3

First Steps in Parenting the Child Who Hurts

Tiddlers and Toddlers

Second Edition

Caroline Archer

Adoption UK

Foreword by Vera Fahlberg

Jessica Kingsley Publishers
London and Philadelphia

First edition published in 1997 by PPIAS (now Adoption UK)

This edition published in the United Kingdom in 1999
by Jessica Kingsley Publishers
116 Pentonville Road
London N1 9JB, UK

and

400 Market Street, Suite 400
Philadelphia, PA 19106, USA

www.jkp.com

Copyright © Adoption UK and Caroline Archer 1999
Illustrations Copyright © Joy Hasler

The right of Adoption UK and Caroline Archer to be identified as authors of this work has been
asserted by them in accordance with the Copyright, Designs and Patents Act 1988.

Library of Congress Cataloging in Publication Data

A CIP catalog record for this book is available from the Library of Congress

British Library Cataloguing in Publication Data

A CIP catalogue record for this book is available from the British Library

ISBN 978 1 85302 801 4

Printed and Bound in Great Britain by
Athenaeum Press, Gateshead, Tyne and Wear

Contents

Still Born

I lie alone
Out of reach,
Too soon to feel
Too soft to touch
Too early to notice
Life passing by;
They know all
And I know nothing.

Inside my swathes
I am overcome
With aching, longing,
Wanting to be close
To be connected
Not left alone
In the safety
Of my own darkness.

Reach out, touch me!
I will not break
Under the weight
Of your faltering care.
Take me close to your heart
Hold me firm and long
For I am adrift,
Lost in the ocean of life.

Can you not sense
The yearning within me
To be contained,
Once more to be one
In the deep warmth
Of your body?
My head is heavy:
I need your support.

And still I lie
Stillborn in the light.
Nobody's child
The doorstep baby,
Wrapped tight and labelled,
Set upon the grey step
Beneath the downcast sky.
Abandoned to the world.

And so I lie. Still.
Quiet as a lamb
Cold as charity
And closer to death.
They cannot hear
My inner cries
Nor sense the urgency
Of my wordless demands.

And, still, I feel the pain
Of that infant realisation
That I am nothing
Cried for no-one
Unheeded, un-needed
Tuned out of touch;
Too young to feel
Too afraid to let go.

Caro Archer June 1993

Acknowledgements

I would like to thank all those friends, family and Adoption UK members alike, who have helped me pull my sometimes off-the-wall thoughts together into some semblance of order. I am very grateful to all the hundreds of Adoption UK members and their families who have shared their hopes, fears and hurts with me over the past few years. In particular I would like to thank Joy Hasler for making my crazy ideas for illustrations a creative reality, Philly Morrall and Lynda Gilbert, who agreed to read and re-read my first drafts, Beth Gibb, Catherine Munroe, Margaret Robertson and Liz Messecar of the Attachment Support Network (now the After Adoption Network) Working Group for their time, energy and encouragement, and the Adoption UK Management Team for its invaluable support. My thanks also go to Dr. Ruth Talbot who so kindly agreed to read and comment on the final draft before publication, despite her increased family commitments.

I give special mention to my husband Allan for his patience and unflappability even in the middle of a crisis, to my children Jenny, Danny, Tom and Jo for their lives and the challenges they continue to offer me, to my grandchildren Chloe, Sophie and Connor for their unquenchable zest for life and to my dog, Olive, who kept my feet warm whilst I sat at the PC. I would also like to thank my own inside children, who have often helped me to know which way to go when things seemed chaotic, and the very special people who have helped us all through some very difficult times. Most of all, I thank each one of you for the many hugs and positive thoughts you have shared with me over the past years.

What is Adoption UK?

Adoption UK (PPIAS until 1999) was formed in 1971 by a group of parents who were involved in adopting children with special needs. Twenty-something years on, membership stands at over 2500 individuals and families. This includes adoptive families with very varied and valuable experiences of adoption, alongside long-term foster carers, prospective adopters and child care practitioners.

Adoption UK is a registered charity which aims to provide information, support and advice for prospective and existing adoptive parents and long-term foster carers. Through its computer-based Experience Resource Bank, ERBIE, and its parent networks, families can also share experiences with each other at every stage of adoption. One of these, the Attachment Support Network (ASN) was established in 1993, as a direct response to members' expressed needs for on-going post-placement support and advice in dealing with a range of behavioural and emotional difficulties within their adoptive families. In 1998, the After Adoption Network (AAN) within Adoption UK replaced the ASN to provide a more inclusive post-adoption support network for *all* adoptive families.

Adoption UK has its office base at 46, The Green, South Bar Street, Banbury, OX16 9AB. Helpline number: 0870 7700 450. Helpdesk email: helpdesk@adoptionuk.org.uk, and has over 120 local volunteer co-ordinators throughout the UK, all of whom are experienced adoptive parents. In addition, adoptive parents who wish to have further opportunities to get in touch with others whose children are showing difficulties around attachment, separation and loss or as a result of other early childhood traumas, may join the AAN and one of a number of regional post-adoption support groups within Adoption UK.

From its inception, adoptive parents have been the prime movers in establishing Adoption UK as a support and information service with effective links with adoption agencies and the ability to raise issues of concern for all adoptive families. Given my great admiration for Adoption UK's 'founding families', particularly Sheilagh and Michael Crawford and Hilary and David Chambers, and my own long-standing links with Adoption UK, it seemed so right to put together and publish *First Steps* as an Adoption UK enterprise. I am particularly pleased that we were able to complete this venture initially in Adoption UK's twenty-fifth anniversary year.

Foreword

First Steps in Parenting the Child Who Hurts: Tiddlers and Toddlers is a 'must have' book for both adoptive parents and for those professionals who help adoptive families forge new family ties. In little more than 100 pages, the author, herself an adoptive parent, addresses a wide variety of very complex topics with a marked sensitivity to the varying needs of children who may have had a wide range of early life experiences. Although in general, the text is easy to read and understand, there is a glossary for those who might be unfamiliar with some of the terminology. References are made to well-established issues as well as to some of the newer research on the impact of early abuse and neglect on brain development. I particularly appreciated the special focus on identifying abnormal arousal patterns and helping the child with these. Parents and professionals alike will value the specific ideas provided for coping with problem behaviours and for building closer family ties.

Dr. Vera Fahlberg M.D.
Forest Heights, Colorado, USA
December 1998

Introduction

Like Topsy, and all children and hedgehogs the world over, this book 'just grew and grew'. It came out of an increasing awareness that many adopted and foster children seemed to struggle with a wide range of developmental issues – at times even when placed as tiny babies. It soon became clear to me that there were many issues relating to adoption, attachment and development which needed to be pulled together into an accessible form for *all* adoptive parents, irrespective of their child's original circumstances, and yet no-one seemed to have done this. Unable to find anyone else willing to undertake this essential task, I decided to 'give it a go' myself.

My use of the phrase 'child who hurts' in the book's title is quite deliberate, for I believe that all children who have been adopted are exposed to psychological pain: at the outset, if they are placed as tiny babies, and as a consequence of their hurtful or abusive experiences, if they are older children. How a child responds to these hurts is very individual and not well understood; some children just seem less resilient than others. However, for many it seems that, by fully acknowledging their hurts, and allowing them to grieve for their losses, they can be helped to move on to a life of greater well-being and fulfilment.

The ambiguity of the title is also intentional, since children who have been hurt may go on to hurt others, especially those who are trying to get close to them. Rather like a hedgehog in fact: soft and delicate on the inside but tough and intensely prickly on the outside, especially when threatened. It also reflects the living dilemma that children and parents alike experience: of being both victim and potential victimiser. Each one of us needs to accept that being hurt and being able to hurt are reciprocal parts of ourselves, which we must bring together and begin to understand. Looking at one without the other increases the likelihood of our repeating our pain in future generations. Facing the whole truth fairly and squarely, without blaming or condemning, offers us a much more realistic and humane way forward.

I have also deliberately chosen to refer to children as 'her' or 'him' interchangeably, since children are both *girls* and *boys* (and not just *boys and girls* as common usage would have it!). On the other hand, I have chosen to avoid the modern idiom of referring to parents as 'primary caregivers', 'significant adults' or, worse still, 'carers' (aren't *all* children and adults 'carers' in some context?). I further elect, at risk of political incorrectness, to use 'mother' to represent the main adult nurturing figure, because I firmly believe that the infant–mother relationship is unique. I do not argue this from a biological essentialist perspective, or because I'm plain old-fashioned. On the contrary, I have struggled long and hard to integrate my feminist stance with what I believe is the baby's own perspective. This, by its very nature, is narrow and informed by the totality of experience in the womb, with *mother*.

That does not by any means leave fathers excluded, or sitting comfortably in their armchairs reading the paper! On the contrary partners, of whatever gender, are precisely that: part of a partnership within which each makes her, or his, vital contribution to the whole. Perhaps in adoption, more than in birth families, there is an opportunity for challenge and exploration of gendered roles, since by definition the young child is forced to relinquish the single most important relationship of her life, with the mother who carried her and gave her life. I believe that this will, inevitably, be a slow metamorphosis, since cultural expectations appear singularly reluctant to adapt to new circumstances. So, whether you are a male or female mother, I wish you well in your chosen role!

Adoption UK has an equal opportunities policy, which extends not only to gender but also to sexual orientation, race, culture, religious belief, class and ability. Although I have deliberately made little direct reference to race, culture and class, there will inevitably be a bias towards 'Britishness' in its widest aspects, since that is the culture from which my own experiences are drawn. I have not excluded any person, or group of persons intentionally in the course of constructing this book as it has always been my expressed wish that everyone should find something within it for themselves. However, I apologise now for any unintentional biases which may remain.

First Steps in Parenting the Child Who Hurts: Tiddlers and Toddlers evolved into its current form as I realised that different people need to know different things at different times, even when thinking about the same child. Hence I hope that **Part One: Coming Home** has something for everyone who has brought, is bringing, or hopes to bring home a baby or young child through adoption. Adoption is different in so many ways from giving birth, and yet it shares many of the inherent joys, sorrows and challenges which we associate with birth parenthood. Balancing the sameness and the differences is a difficult task for each of us and is pivotal to our children's well-being.

Part Two: New Beginnings looks at early child development, with the emphasis on that additional adoption dimension, whilst **Part Three: When Things Don't Seem Quite Right** considers some possible indications that things may not be going as smoothly for your child and your family as you might hope or expect. In **Part Four: The Effects of Trauma on Attachment**

and Development I have attempted to summarise as simply as possible what is currently known about the traumatic effects of early separations, losses, abuse and neglect from both the psychological and physiological perspectives. The text remains complex but I hope that the *Glossary*, which covers unfamiliar terms used throughout the book, will help you.

I have tried, in **Part Five: Getting Back on Track**, to set out a variety of suggestions for handling a wide range of potential 'problems' which may come up for you and your child sooner or later. It is hoped that your child will not display the majority of these at any one time! They are based broadly on my own, and adoptive parent friends', personal experiences within our own families. All our lives might have run a good deal smoother if we had understood more clearly the hurts which underlay much of our children's behaviour and, although I firmly believe that it is never too late, there are clearly many advantages in getting to grips with them as early as possible. As one of my colleagues wrote recently, 'I only wish someone had given me this sort of information when my son was small.'

Part Six: Special Difficulties Within Your Family begins to address some particular issues you may come up against in your family, which may be directly related to your adoptive family status. These include life-story work, contact, siblings and disability: the way these important issues are planned and managed can have dramatic effects on our children's understanding of themselves and their relationships with others.

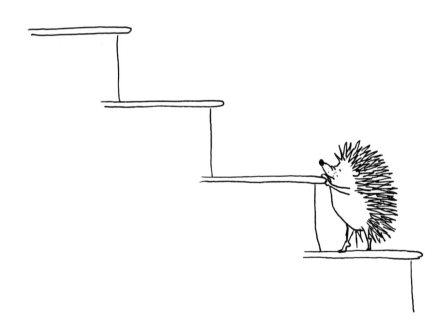

Finally, I consider some elements of **The Spiritual Dimension** in **Part Seven**. I hope you will take only what you need from this, and indeed every other section. Since we are all unique, there will inevitably be aspects with which you do not identify, or with which you do not feel comfortable. I trust that you will set these aside, perhaps for future consideration or discussion.

Since *First Steps in Parenting the Child Who Hurts: Tiddlers and Toddlers* is intended primarily for adoptive and foster parents, I have kept references within the text to a minimum. I hope that those which remain will not put readers off, or leave you feeling frustrated. A list of such references as there are, along with suggestions for further reading, may be found at the end of the book.

Next Steps in Parenting the Child Who Hurts: Tykes and Teens

There is a sequel to *First Steps* known as *Next Steps in Parenting the Child Who Hurts: Tykes and Teens*. This is a guide for adoptive parents of older children. Adoption is a life-long process and I hope that these two books will contribute in a small way to your family's experiences and that you, in your turn, may contribute to the knowledge and lives of future adoptees and their families. You are welcome to write to me, through Adoption UK, with your comments, questions and insights.

Coming Home

This is a book about you and your adopted little one, or the baby or young child you hope to have. It has been put together to give you a flying start as a special family, recognising that the life tasks of adoptive parents and their children are not always the same as those of birth parents. It is hoped that it will help to guide you through the early years, drawing on your natural expertise and building up your confidence to be '***good enough***' parents for your child. That, as D.W. Winnicott, the eminent British child psychiatrist said over thirty years ago, is all you need to be: ***good enough!*** (*Words in bold italics may be found in the* **Glossary** *at the end of this book.*)

You may know very little of your baby's history, in the womb, immediately after her birth and in the period before she came to you. **Do try to find out as much as you can about the social and clinical circumstances of her early life, since it can help you to feel closer and more attuned to your little one, and enable you to help her make sense of her experiences. Adoption UK has produced a very useful booklet,** *A Checklist for Prospective Adopters,* which lists some of the questions you may wish to ask and which is available free to all Adoption UK members. Be patient but persistent and don't be afraid to go back to social workers, medical staff and previous carers and ask more awkward questions, as and when you need.

Avoiding Difference

Do all you can to find out about your baby's daily experiences and routines from the people who are most likely to know. These could include birth family members, foster parents, hospital nursing staff and residential workers in the children's home or orphanage where your child was staying. It isn't usually the people at the top, or the intermediaries such as social workers and lawyers, who can give you this sort of detail: it is the 'hands-on' caregivers whom you need to get to know.

You may well not agree with the way things were being done, and have great ideas of your own about caring for your young child when he comes home, **but it is vitally important that you keep as much of his environment and experience the same as usual, at least in the short term.** Try to keep to the same rhythms and routines, use the same clothing and bedding, milk formula and other foods. That way your child's home-coming will be as smooth and as unstressed as you can make it.

Of course, if you are aware that your young child was neglected, badly treated or subjected to painful medical procedures, you won't want to allow those hurtful patterns to continue. You should remember however that they may be the *only* experiences your child has had and that there is comfort in even painful familiarity. Hence it will be vital that you work even harder to maintain some of the better aspects of his care as the daily framework for his new life with you, whilst introducing healthier, comforting experiences as soon as you can.

Keep in mind that smell is very important to very young children, since it accesses directly that part of the brain (the ***limbic system***), which is concerned with memory and with selective awareness. Try to bring home with your new baby some of the blankets or clothes she had in her previous home. They will still carry familiar smells with them. Do not wash them but keep them close to your child, so that something of her old environment stays with her during this stressful time of transition. The smell of your car, for example, may continue to make her very anxious, due to its previous associations with sudden change. You should try to make sure that some of the old familiar smells and textures go with your baby wherever she goes, for at least the first few months after she comes home.

It is important to sensitise your child very gradually to your touch, smell, voice, face and other sense perceptions when she comes to you. Bear in mind that everything in her life has been changed, seemingly without meaning. So go easy on any further changes in her life for the foreseeable future. Even a switch in washing powder, or in the weight and feel of her duvet at home, may emphasise the apparent chaos in her life. Do all you can to stick to the same milk powder, bottles and teats, or similar solid foods and feeding implements, and try to keep to a similar feeding schedule in the early weeks after you bring your infant home. Food is a very basic need, and has early and powerfully lasting *associations* with comfort and well-being; therefore it is particularly important to ease your baby's transition into your family in this area.

Try as hard as you can to avoid all unnecessary travel over the first few months and postpone any further home moves for the next few years if at all possible! Think hard before you arrange your holidays away. You certainly deserve a break and a change but try to find a balance between your own needs and your young child's need for continuity and sameness in the early years. Similarly, if you are considering further additions to your family, take your time and give this little one the emotional space he will need to feel secure. **Home will come to feel like home to him very much sooner and more permanently if it is predictable and unchanging and you are there just for him.**

Remember that starting nursery may still be too much for some rising four-year-olds. Be prepared to keep your child with you at home just a little longer or to find a playgroup or nursery where you will be welcomed with her. Let her take her 'blankie' with her and come back for her on time, or even a little early, since she has a heightened sense of *abandonment* and may need extra reassurances about your reliability. **Once you have firmly established your permanence, and she has learned to trust that you will always come back for her, she will be so much more firmly independent and confident in herself, in every way.**

Making the Difference

Having emphasised the importance of keeping things just as they were in the short term, to make your baby's change less disturbing for him, there will be things you may wish to do differently right from the start. Remember that there is already one major difference in his life now: **you — and you can make all the difference in the world!**

You should take it as read that your baby will need extra nurturing in the first few days, weeks and months of her coming home to you. Being aware of the possibility of difficulties, and being ready to relate dynamically with your baby, can enhance your chances of establishing healthy patterns of relating early on. Good early *attachment* provides the best foundation for your vulnerable youngster, (Winnicott's '*psychological containment*'), and can help to lessen your baby's levels of distress, which could be vital to her future well-being and overall development.

It makes good sense to handle your baby as if she were premature or new-born, whatever her age on coming to you. Give yourself plenty of time to begin to learn more about each other. This may well include being very firm with all your doting relatives and excited friends who want to share your good fortune. They can wait; you and your baby cannot. **Pregnant women and babies in the womb spend nine months getting to know each other: you both have some catching up to do!** In the longer term it may take your young child quite a bit longer to feel safe when left with other people, such as babysitters, even for a brief period, since this may *trigger* distressing feelings about the initial separation(s).

Pick up, hold, nuzzle, smell, rock, stroke, gaze at, whisper and sing to your baby endlessly. **As long as you are relaxed and remain sensitive to her needs for periodic rest and quiet, this cannot be overdone.** Your little one will be doing her part too, becoming familiar with your smell, your body movements, your voice patterns, your inner body rhythms.

Set aside as much time as you can to share skin-to-skin contact. Tuck her (in nappy only, or less) inside your biggest, baggiest tee-shirt and relax, inside a warm blanket in your favourite armchair. Your heart beat, your body warmth and your relaxed breathing will all help her to feel soothed and secure and she will begin to learn to *regulate* her own basic body functions. You are giving her the opportunity to get as close as she can, to be held and to connect. In a sense you are trying to re-create the initial bonding which should take place between mother and baby in the womb. In some countries this way of nurturing, known as 'Kangaroo Care', is routinely recommended for the most vulnerable, premature babies and has been shown to be more effective than any state-of-the-art intensive care interventions.

If it feels right for you, it may be possible to suckle your adopted infant, most probably as a supplement to formula feeding. You don't have to have given birth yourself in the past, or even produce milk, to make this a positive experience for you both. Even when this does not seem an option, **allowing your baby to lie snugly against your breast is a very special way of nurturing: you are re-creating the most natural body position for your infant, stimulating the earliest developmental connections between you, and bringing your baby, literally, into your heart.** It is a wonderful close feeling, which you both richly deserve, over and over again. (More information about suckling and breast-feeding adopted infants can be obtained from La Leche League. For the address and also a contact list of adoptive mothers who suckled or breast-fed their babies, get in touch with Adoption UK direct.)

It can be enormously helpful to get hold of a good, comfortable front-to-front contact sling. There are several excellent models on the market but do make sure you try it out in the store, for comfort and manoeuvrability, before you buy! Alternatively you could stick to 'Kangaroo Care', or wrap your little one in a Welsh shawl or African cloth sling. A small baby cannot push you away in a sling the way he may in your arms; you are also left with both hands free to caress, stroke or tickle your baby or to hold your older child's hand, turn the pages of a book, hold a cup of tea or the phone, stir the gravy or even (!) manage a few light, essential chores.

When you need to use a pram or pushchair, try to find a reversible one which allows your young baby to look at you, so that you can continue to make eye contact whilst you are out of direct touch. As your child grows older and begins to show more interest in the outside world you can turn the pushchair outwards and keep in touch through your voice and through occasional physical contact. The new baby carriers which strap into the front seat of your car will allow you to maintain close proximity, face-to-face contact and connection with a young infant, whilst you drive – but beware of safety warnings on some cars with passenger seat air bags. Do remember that even a short car ride may be stressful to a baby who has already experienced several life moves, so anything you can do to minimise her distress will be valuable (see also 'Avoiding Difference', pages 18–19).

Set aside regular quiet times when you and your baby, and growing child, can spend time together doing nothing more than being together. Establishing *'holding time'* is an excellent way of doing this (see section on 'Safe Holding' in Part 5, page 69) and our recommended reading list for more information. It is in those intimate, quiet times that you and your young child can really get to know each other and open special lines of communication at many different levels. Continue these special times through the pre-school years and into the 'latency' (school-age) period; your child will go on needing 'top-ups' of quiet closeness to counterbalance the stresses of his growing independence and the pressures of his day.

If everything feels right between you and your child, then carry on enjoying her, secure in the knowledge that you are growing closer to each other in a healthy way. **If, on the other hand, your baby's responses do not feel right to you, for whatever reason, trust your intuition**. As you get to know your baby you are becoming highly attuned to her most vital needs and expressions, and you are in a unique position to pick up on potential problems that other, more 'expert' people may not. Simply by spending more time with your baby than anyone else you have the advantage, if only you trust your inner feelings and act on them.

New Beginnings: Early Child Development

It can be very helpful, as parents of new little ones, and as parents of new but older 'little ones', to turn to one of the numerous outlines of young child development which are currently available (see the Adoption UK booklist for some suggestions). Below are some simple developmentally based questions which may be particularly relevant to infants and toddlers who have experienced the *traumatic hurts* of very early separations, losses or inconsistencies of care. They are set out 'bottom up', in ascending order of development, to help you get an idea of 'where your child is' after she comes home to you and what extra help you may give her in this vital early period.

- **Does your baby appear to gain relief and comfort from you tending to her most basic needs, such as being held, being smiled at and talked to and being fed, watered and changed regularly?**

  If you sense there is anything not quite right here, this may be where you will need to begin.

- **Is he easily startled, for example by a sudden loud noise, as a new-born baby would be?**

  It could be vital to take note of any specific or unusual responses from your baby.

- **Does your baby/little one take an interest in your face, exploring it with her eyes or her fingers?**

  This stage is most common in the first six months of life but may persist where a baby has experienced separations or inconsistencies.

- **Does your infant try to get your attention by 'wooing' you with his body movements, facial expressions and eyes?**

  This stage begins at around eight weeks and is usually very well established by six to seven months of age. It is part of the give and take of close relationships. There may be cause for concern if this behaviour has not developed and you may need to work harder to encourage her *reciprocal* responses.

- **Has she begun to establish a pattern of sleeping and wakefulness?**

  A baby who has been moved may take longer to settle into a comfortable rhythm. She may react by excessive waking or sleep and you may need to work out additional ways of developing her sense of consistency and security.

- **How does your baby relate to other people?**

  Normally developing infants can recognise, and show preference for, one adult over others in their first weeks of life. If your baby seems as comfortable moving from one pair of arms to another as he does relating exclusively to you, this *may* point to some difficulties.

- **Does he respond to your smiles and chuckles with something similar of his own? Does your baby take an interest in other people's faces?**

  This is a more complex stage of development, which does not usually take place without him first recognising, and becoming fascinated with, the face of the *'mothering figure'* (you!)

- **Has your baby begun to prefer to face away from you for movement and exploration?**

  This should be a normal developmental step towards independence and exploration at around six months, once the total dependency stage has been successfully worked through. If your child either moves away from you *too soon*, or does not want to do this as he develops, you may have to work harder at establishing basic security.

- **Does your baby look back to you for reassurance if picked up by someone else, or is at a distance from you?**
  Stranger anxiety is *said* to be observable from around six to seven months, although even very young babies may show a preference for a particular person almost from birth. At this stage your baby may become less comfortable with close contact with others and will look to you for comfort and assurance that things will be O.K. This *'referent looking'* should also be seen as your baby becomes more mobile and shuffles, crawls or toddles away from you.
  He will need to 'check in' regularly that you are still there, if he is to establish 'object constancy', (see also Part 1: Coming Home.)

- **Does your youngster play or have his attention directed elsewhere for increasing periods without distress, focusing his attention more on play-things and other people and less on you?**

  He may be using *transitional objects*: familiar items which can serve as constant reminders of your continuing presence. Or is he still in the earlier developmental stage of needing to look back at you frequently for security? Gentle encouragement, understanding and time may be needed to move him on.

- **Is she able to manage times of quiet, perhaps beginning to self-soothe through gentle rocking or thumb-sucking? Can she also enjoy times of noise and activity, or do her activity levels seem frequently too low or too frenetic?**

  All toddlers may withdraw or go wild at times, but some can be quite over the top. This may be due to heightened anxieties and a weakened ability to *soothe* themselves or be *soothed*. You may have to work harder to establish a more normal rhythm of life.

- **Has he reached the 'terrible twos', where greater independence and greater frustrations are evident?**

  Whilst all toddlers may struggle with this balance, a youngster who displays repeated tantrums, impulsive behaviour or expressions of aggression may need extra support and safe containment. (See subsequent sections on 'Grounding' (p.66), 'Tantrums' (p.74), 'Aggression' (p.78) and 'Siblings' (p.91) in Parts 5 and 6.)

- **Does your toddler seem to be bumping into things, or breaking things more than you would expect as he becomes more mobile?**

Accident proneness in young children can be an indication of poor motor co-ordination (*dyspraxia*). In older children there may be some intentional destructiveness or *self-harm* as a result of earlier *trauma*.

It is important to emphasise that you should always seek advice from your health visitor or doctor if you have any real worries. If after talking to them you still do not feel fully reassured, ask for a second opinion and a complete paediatric examination.

However, it is also vital that you are aware of the potentially damaging effects on your child's development, and ability to form good *attachments*, of being subjected to any unnecessary, intrusive medical investigations. These may be experienced as further *traumatic* distress. Always check with your doctor or health visitor that any proposed procedure is really necessary and do your best to ensure that you remain with your child at all times, to provide closeness, reassurance and sympathy. Be honest, always acknowledge that even a routine vaccination may be very painful and talk your little one quietly through the experience. In that way you will validate your infant's experience and you will not have broken her trust.

After you have obtained adequate reassurances about your child's general health, you can feel free to begin your own developmental programme if you wish. Just as the conductive educators at the Peto Institute may physically lead children with cerebral palsy through their movements towards developmental health, so we can psychologically and physically lead our children through their feelings and movements towards greater emotional and developmental health. Remember that the Peto therapists verbalise and name every movement that the child is making, so that she will become consciously aware of her actions.

It is vital to talk our children, however small, through their body experiences and body movements, as well as their feelings, so that they may begin to identify them and subsequently gain greater *self-awareness* and conscious *self-control*.

When Things Don't Seem Quite Right

!?¡¿

Most babies will respond positively to being picked up and cuddled. They enjoy physical contact and take comfort from having their basic needs for touch, warmth, nourishment, movement and *soothing* sound, met consistently. **You may have a potential problem if your baby does not respond in this way.** He may, for example, go stiff and actively push away from you when you handle him, or scream in distress. Obviously it is a good idea to check out all the usual reasons for his distress, such as needing to be fed or to have his nappy changed. If none of these seems to be the case, and your baby seems not to be able to relax with you or relate to you, you may have a baby with some potential *sensori-motor*, *developmental* or *attachment* problems.

Some of us have ourselves had babies and young children placed with us who have been very difficult, unhappy, uncomfortable with touch, sound or movement, or who seemed unusually unresponsive. From our own experiences, and with hindsight, we realise that we did not always know how to help our babies well enough. By providing you with information and suggestions, which are supported by current theories of *attachment*, *development* and *trauma*, we hope we will give you the choice many of us feel we lacked. **It will always be your decision whether to act, or to wait and see; only you will know your child well enough to make that choice.**

Below we have included some real-life descriptions, from adoptive parents, of their babies and toddlers. They may begin to ring bells straight away with some of you. This may mean that you will want to learn more about ways of easing your little one's life-path. (Some specific suggestions for helping your child are outlined in Part 5: Getting Back on Track, beginning on page 48.)

These descriptions have been deliberately kept short. It is hoped that they will offer you some snap-shots of how some of our children were in their early years. All of the children were placed in their families before their second birthdays.

> *He came to us at six months. He just did not like being held and would push himself away from me. He seemed always to be banging his head on the door-post as I carried him from one room to another.*

> *Our son was only a few months old but he screamed and screamed almost non-stop. He reacted particularly badly to any change: like seeing someone in the street whom he knew from in the house.*

> *He didn't smile and almost never cried, even when he woke up from his nap. I would go up to his cot and he would look at me blankly, as if he didn't know me.*

> *We had our baby from four months. She never seemed to sleep during the day and demanded constant amusement. She woke up several times every night – until she was five years old.*

> *It felt like toddler tantrums at four to six months old. He would work himself up into an unpacifiable rage. There didn't seem anything we could do.*

> *Our second baby came home at nine months. She clung to me like a little monkey. I couldn't even go to the loo on my own. For weeks and weeks she would start to scream the moment my husband came into the room.*

He didn't seem to notice me. One day, when he was still very small, I passed him to a friend so that I could answer the phone. He just kept his eyes fixed on the bottle and didn't come up for air until every drop was gone.

I had to unpick all the labels from her baby clothes because they seemed to irritate her so much. I still have to be careful with materials and washing powders or she just wriggles and fidgets and pulls them off.

She would want to hold the bottle herself, from early on. She would get very upset if I insisted on holding her and feeding her. She didn't even seem to come up for air and screamed blue murder when it was all gone.

My little girl didn't seem able to chew. She would collect food up in her mouth like a hamster until we encouraged her to spit it out. This went on and on. She is now in her teens and she is still a very fussy eater. She often starves herself, then binges.

Our little girl was late walking. When she did learn she held her hands out to the sides, palms facing forward, thumbs bent inwards. If she fell she did not try to break her fall. Inevitably, she often had cuts and bruises on her nose and forehead!

He was nearly one and a half when he came home to us. He wasn't walking but would crawl round at full tilt. He rushed from toy to toy without ever really paying attention to anything, or anybody. He didn't seem to know how to play.

Our toddler was terrified of certain objects. He would become very distressed by simple things like balloons. He wouldn't go into playgroup when they had the big inflatable ball out.

If she couldn't have something straight away she would become frantic, biting the back of her own hand as tears poured down her face. She would go puce with rage.

Going out in the wind was a nightmare. He hated his hair being blown about. He also detested having his hair washed and would scream and scream at bath time.

He calmed down a lot when he learned to walk. He would just turn and walk away from me. A few minutes later he would have calmed down. He didn't seem able to be comforted by anyone.

She would sit there in the trolley charming all the other shoppers, her big blue eyes shining. But she would never do that for me. She always seemed to be looking away.

Some babies and very young children may be over- or under-responsive to touch, sound, movement, odours, visual images and light, or the tastes and textures of foods: that is they are *hyper-* or *hypo-sensitive* in one or more of their *sensory* channels, including movement. For many reasons, including prenatal exposure to drugs, alcohol, poor nutrition and physical, auditory and emotional *traumas* in the womb, the baby may seem unable to respond to pleasurable experiences. Since all babies, at this early stage of development, experience and make sense of the world, predominantly through their bodies and their senses, **a baby with these *sensori-motor* sensitivities may have difficulties relating to her environment comfortably and in establishing healthy *attachment* relationships.**

As a parent, being aware of the increased likelihood of difficulties for adopted little ones can help you to minimise the potential problems, in both the short, and the longer term. However, **do not allow yourself to become over-anxious or this will inevitably communicate itself to your baby.** Anxiously gazing at your baby may raise her heart and respiratory rates and cause her to try to look away. Allan Schore contends that the *'gaze avert'* response allows reduction in basic stress levels: that is the baby can relax and feel calm and comfortable. It can become problematic, however, if the baby comes to use this strategy frequently to avoid eye contact and opportunities for close relating.

In the Adoption UK leaflet *Adoption, Attachment and Development* we highlight some areas of your child's **attachment** and early development which are particularly important and which may give you some early indications of your child's level of well-being. These are listed below. **Do please remember that any difficulties in individual areas will not, on their own, suggest that your child is likely to have significant *attachment* or *developmental* difficulties.**

Touch	over- or under-sensitive to cuddling, stroking, bathing, tickling
Eye Contact	avoids, or is reluctant to look into, your face directly, or may seem to look through you
Sensory Responses	over-sensitivity to sensory experience, e.g. exaggerated response to sudden sounds or movements; or specific lack of response to such experiences
Sound	over- or under-sensitive to everyday sound, including your voice
Movement	frenetic, hyperactive, on the go all the time; or inhibited, immobile or stiff
Responsiveness	over-reaction to new stimuli, to changes or to human approaches; or noticeable lack of response to new or familiar situations
Muscle Tone	very tense muscle tone; or poor muscle tone, such as excessive dribbling; poor gross or fine motor skills
Crying	crying for extended periods, inconsolable or attempting to *self-soothe*; or lack of tears or distress where you would normally expect this
Feeding	excessive demands for food, gorging, vomiting; or poor appetite, poor feeding, sucking and/or chewing
Sleep	very difficult to settle, wakeful, *hypervigilant*; or sleeping for excessive periods, or as a response to stress
Irritability	difficult to console, easily disturbed by even small changes; or apparently indifferent to much that goes on
Fear	shows unusual or excessive fearfulness, or is apparently not afraid of anything or anyone
Vocalisation	constant chattering, which may be repetitive; or lack of babbling or vocalisation, even in response to playful encouragement
Stranger Anxiety	will go 'happily' to anyone; or appears to be comfortable with no-one, especially after the first six months of life.

Again, it is always a good idea to speak to your doctor or health visitor first, if you have any specific concerns. If you still have anxieties about your child, you could ask for a referral to a paediatric clinical psychologist, developmental neuro-psychologist, paediatrician, occupational therapist or paediatric speech and language therapist. Resist the 'anxious mother' label at all costs: you may need to be persistent to get what you need for your child. **Most important, keep in mind that you will (soon) know your little one better than anyone else and already have many of the necessary skills to help your youngster's development back on course.**

If you do decide to set out on the developmental journey with your child, try to make sure that you have plenty of fun! **You will also need to find time, outside of your little one's life, to let off steam, to take care of your own needs and to get sufficient rest.** It is vital that you approach your child calmly, lovingly and patiently. You must respect her individuality and her need for occasional *switching off* times, and avoid giving her any messages of frustration, failure or punishment, as her *self-esteem* may have already been compromised.

Your little one will benefit best from the time you give her if she feels relaxed and accepted and is not over-tired. Try to work out her 'best times', when she seems happiest being nursed, stroked, 'worked with' and then capitalise on it. You may find that she is more responsive in one sensory dimension than another. You can gradually introduce those elements she finds most trying alongside her favourites, until she can tolerate and even enjoy them.

This can be a particular challenge where your child appears over-sensitive, disinterested, avoidant, rejecting, over-impulsive, destructive or aggressive, or all of these within a matter of minutes! **It is O.K. to feel hurt, angry, frustrated or sad about your little one but it is NEVER O.K. to act these feelings out towards her.** It has helped some of us to create fantasies of the most bizarre, or the most dastardly, thing we might dream of doing and have a good chuckle over this with our partners or friends in private. Then we can let it go and get back to being loving, understanding, tolerant, consistent (even in our inconsistencies) and containing parents for our children!

Throughout *First Steps*, the focus is primarily on strategies designed to enhance ***attachment*** and overall development. **The aim is to help the young child become alert and able to pay good attention, without becoming over-stimulated or over-anxious.** This happens initially through the physical closeness of parent and child and through mutually enjoyable activities which open up the child's senses and ability to learn. **Equally important are experiences of quiet and calm,** which are initially experienced from an outside source (the parent's example) and gradually become part of the child's inner pattern of *self-regulation*. The eventual goal is for the child to develop his own stable mechanisms for *self-stimulating* (becoming *alert* and focused) and *self-soothing* (finding an inner security and peace). **This ability to alter levels of physical and emotional *arousal* is fundamental to the child's sense of well-being and his ability to make sense of his world.**

The Effects of Trauma on Attachment and Development

Knowing more about your young child's intellectual, physical and emotional development may help you in your day-to-day routines. However, if you want to skip this section, that's fine. You can get along pretty well without it. Perhaps one day you'll choose to come back to it – or maybe not! If and when you feel ready for it: read on.

Some of these developmental concepts, and their interconnections, are very complex and many of the terms in common usage in this area may be unfamiliar to you. Where it is possible, substitutions or translations of technical terms have been made and a *Glossary* of the words shown in italics is provided at the end of the book. However it has not always been possible to simplify, without risk of losing some of the essential meaning.

Tiffany Field (1985) defined attachment as 'a relationship that develops between two or more organisms as their behavioral and *physiological* systems become *attuned* to each other'. Clearly, it is through an intense and intimate relationship with the *mothering figure(s)* that these essential biological and psychological connections (*synchronic attunements*) can take place. Subsequently, security and trust can become established and the young child can begin to gain a *sense of self.*

The Importance of the Senses

We tend to think of the senses in terms of the 'famous five' – touch, taste, smell, sound and vision, hence with the term *sensori-motor* we include all these, plus the element of movement. However it may be far more useful to consider the infant's development of *sense of self* both in psychological-emotional terms and in terms of awareness of body functions, sensations, positions and movements. Good attachment experiences lead to a good sense of self: 'I know who I am in relation to those around me. I feel good about myself and I know how to make sense of my inner feelings'. Healthy, early infantile experience also involves *proprioception* an awareness of body parts in relation to each other and in space, and *praxis* the ability to conceive, plan and execute body movements.

Achieving the intimacy and mutuality of dependency and interaction implicit to the attachment relationship has been shown to bring about greater *neurological organisation,* at a very critical time. In the *brain stem,* which is responsible for *homeostatic* regulation of heart and breathing rates and of body temperature, this begins in the womb and continues in the period immediately after birth. The *critical developmental period* for the *mid brain,* including the 'emotional' *limbic system,* is during the first three years of life, which includes pregnancy. During this time, the infant's systems of regulating alertness and the ability to focus on important experiences in the world (*modulation of arousal*) and daily patterns of eating and sleeping (*diurnal rhythms*) are set in place. The limbic system has direct links to our *cortical,* or thinking, brain and plays a major part both in recognising and managing emotions and in developing attachments. It is the first location for the processing of perceptions in the areas of sensation and movement.

Like the proverbial house upon the sand, establishing a fully functional thinking brain (the *cortical neurological system*) without an intact mid brain and limbic system is problematic. In fact, the ability to regulate levels of alertness and focus (first through intimacy, *soothing and stimulation* from the mother figure and then through *self-soothing and self-stimulation*) forms the cornerstone of the child's ability to learn. Martha Welch (1994) contends that greatest learning takes place in the 'quiet alert' period immediately following 'holding time' (see Safe Holding in Part 5: Getting Back on Track on page 69.) Through close, body-to-body contact, the infant has a vital opportunity to 'tune into' his loving mother and reach an optimal state of relaxed alertness.

Since babies organise their neurological systems, perceptions and understanding around what they experience, particularly during these critical developmental periods, it is vital that we as parents do our utmost to provide our little ones with compensatory, learning experiences as soon as we can. Over time, all the infant's myriad of raw experiences are registered in different sensory areas, categorised and committed to memory in different parts of the brain. Gradually these innumerable separate *sensori-motor* experiences become more or less *associated*, or *integrated*, so that the child acquires a competent, holistic sense of self in mind and body, a functional template by which she will live her life.

For a child where things do not go well in these *critical formative periods*, the sense of *self* is frequently compromised. If his basic needs are not met, he may never learn to identify hunger, thirst, discomfort or pain or to associate these sensations with *gratification*, the means and sources of relief. He will certainly not learn to trust in his caregivers and his environment to meet his needs. His needs may remain *dissociated* from his conscious awareness and yet form the driving force for his actions. If he experiences repeated intense pain or fear or abuse, or further separations this can seriously compromise his ability to *modulate* his *arousal levels*, which in turn makes it unlikely that he will be able to make sense of, and learn from, his later experiences of life.

Trauma, especially such intense, early childhood trauma, has been shown to lead to the increased likelihood of *dissociations*. There may be dissociations of awareness in different sensory modalities, dissociations between *implicit* (pre- and non-verbal) memory and *explicit* (expressive, narrative) memory, dissociations between brain stem, mid brain, limbic system and cortical areas of the brain and dissociations between the logic and language functions of the left brain hemisphere and the intuitive, holistic functions of the right. The sense of self, past and present, may remain fragmented, patterns of thinking remain confused and behaviours persist over which the individual appears to have little conscious control. A lack of associations between mind and body is also common.

This could be compared with a computer system where one area does not communicate information to another, or allow analysis of all in-coming or out-going data within the entire system. The computer may be able to perform simple, linked functions but will not be able to carry out complex functions, may make serious functional errors and may ultimately crash. These breaks in the circuitry will need to be identified and made good for optimal functioning to be made possible.

It is becoming clearer that attachment and a child's development in every sphere are firmly linked, through the mediating factor of *trauma*. This is an exciting new area of research at the cutting edge of knowledge and, as yet, we do not have all the answers. What we can say with some certainty is that the concept of trauma can help us to understand much of our adopted children's life narrative. **The term** *trauma* **is taken from the Greek, meaning a wound, and has been extended to encompass both physical and psychological** *hurts*. It is very appropriate that Nancy Verrier (1994) adopted the title *The Primal Wound* for her ground-breaking volume, in which she acknowledged and described the lasting *psychic* pain that can result from very early separations.

There is as yet no objective measure of *trauma*, no regulated instrument which can measure an experience and predict with great certainty what effects it will have on any given individual. Even within the same family, two children may experience and react to the same tragedy, such as the sudden death of a parent, in quite different ways. Researchers are only just beginning to test out the protective factors against, and unique vulnerabilities of human beings to, adversity. **However, almost all would agree that adverse experiences are likely to be more damaging if the individual has not developed a strong sense of self, has not established a firm network of attachment figures upon whom he may rely, and does not have the cognitive capacities to make sense of what is happening.**

When we also realise that the vast majority of human development takes place during infancy and that organisation within and between the sense organs, nervous system and brain is set in place as a direct result of what is experienced, then it will be clear that in many ways very young children are at the greatest risk of disturbance to their developmental processes. Old arguments, that the baby has no ability to think or speak about an event and will therefore not experience early trauma, are being firmly countered by many *paediatricians* and *neuro-physiologists*. Research clinicians such as Bessel van der Kolk (1996), John Brière (1992) and Bruce Perry (1993) are beginning to demonstrate, unequivocally, the direct effects of overwhelming experience on the development of the brain, central and *autonomic nervous systems*. Just as the virus rubella (German measles) can have devastating effects on the foetus during the first three months of pregnancy and yet pass almost unnoticed in a young adult, so an apparently minor physical or *psychological trauma* to a developing infant can have devastating long-term effects.

We often think of arousal, like stress, in a negative context: that is that stress and arousal should be avoided or minimised. In reality our bodies are programmed to function well under certain limits of external and internal pressure. Too little physical stress from the outside could mean our bodies would not stand up. We would be a mess of floppy jelly. Similarly, too little arousal on the inside would make it difficult for us to remain alert, to pick out and react in appropriate ways to the important pieces from the masses of information which hit our senses all the time. Most of us don't notice, for example, that background hubbub as we work, because we are selectively paying attention to what we are doing.

An infant is not born with *selective attention*, it is something that is learned over the years, from experience. *Modulation of arousal* is about the ability to be alert enough to pay attention, and to be focused enough to pick out the important messages bombarding our senses, our brains and our nervous systems, without sensory or *neuro-physiological* overload. It is also about being able to deal with feelings and emotions and then being able to come back to 'normal' once the experience is over. Babies and young children learn about modulation of arousal from the people around them. For children who experience mostly comfort, security and consistency, this transition to healthy *self-regulation* is not problematic. For little ones who have not had these opportunities, who have experienced sensory or emotional overload through some degree of trauma, the story becomes more complex. (Please refer to Figure 4.2 on page 25.)

On a psychological level, *trauma* may affect the individual's ability to feel safe, to trust other people and to feel that they have any influence over their destiny. On a physical level it can alter the individual's ability to *modulate arousal* and to regulate basic bodily functions such as heart rate, breathing rate and sleep patterns, as well as emotions such as anger and fear. The child's experience has been so overwhelmingly stressful, or prolonged, that the normal ability to return to a comfortable basal level of functioning (*homoeostasis*) is compromised. The traumatised individual may remain in constant *physiological* readiness for the next danger, prone to impulsive action without reflection, or to social withdrawal. She may continue to feel totally unconnected and alone. For a child this is magnified by her relative lack of compensating, positive experience and her relative inability to make sense of what has happened to her.

Very young babies experience the world in *stochastic* chunks, that is as all or nothing events, without the ability to keep in mind any other possibility. Hence when mother leaves baby on her own even for a few minutes, the baby's experience is that she is gone for ever. The separation appears infinite and life threatening. A baby only gradually learns to move from one feeling state to another, and to develop an understanding of such concepts as *object constancy*, that objects including people do not disappear when not in touch, sight, smell or earshot, through experiencing her mother as consistently present. In time, through the modulating effects of soothing and stimulation from her nurturing caregiver, through sensitively moderated, progressive separations suited to her developmental maturity and comforting *transitional objects* such as 'blankies', this process is consolidated and she can tolerate more lengthy separations and distresses without becoming overwhelmed. **One of the most lasting and profound effects of early trauma is the interference with the developmental learning process of** *self-regulation.*

Thus, new born babies who are separated from their birth mothers soon after birth are likely to experience the loss as total abandonment, whether the separation is temporary, due perhaps to medical interventions designed to keep them alive, or permanent, due to relinquishment for adoption. In either case the baby loses touch with everything she has come to know in the womb: the harmonisation (*synchronic attunement*) to mother's heart, respiratory and temperature patterns, her tone of voice, her body movements, her rhythms of night and day (*diurnal rhythmicity*) are all interrupted. She experiences only abandonment. Since the baby has none of the suggested protective factors against trauma in place at this time, this initial traumatic experience may very powerfully influence all her future perceptions of the world.

Hence it is now becoming clear that babies and very young children may be far more vulnerable to adversity in many situations than their older counterparts. The *neuro-hormones* which mediate emotion are known to cross the placenta, so that a baby in the womb may be exposed to physiological stress even before birth. Whilst the baby in utero has no way of knowingly labelling the flood of emotions which may reach her, her developing *neurological system* may be overwhelmed. For example, if the mother is in a heightened state of anxiety over an extended period (perhaps worrying how she can tell her partner or parents she is pregnant, or how to carry on concealing the pregnancy from her family and friends), her own stress hormones will also have a distressing influence on the baby she is carrying.

The ability to alter levels of alertness and response to stress (to *modulate neuro-physiological arousal*) is still weak in very young organisms, so that a baby may remain in a *traumatising, aroused* state for extended periods. This, in its turn, may make her a more irritable, restless baby, causing her mother additional discomfort during the pregnancy, and compounding her own distress. **This state of *over-arousal* may persist uninterrupted into the early weeks of her life and interfere with early, innate *attachment* behaviours.**

The relationship between *trauma* and *attachment* can be reciprocal. Attachments can facilitate the essential modulation of basic functioning, help a child make sense of the world and protect her from feeling overwhelmed, out of control and alone. Conversely, trauma can shatter the trust of even the most healthily attached individual, at least temporarily. *Physiologically*, **the experience of trauma leads to dramatic changes in the ability to respond, which for the most vulnerable, including very young children, are not readily brought back to normal.** The persisting, heightened state of arousal may not only continue to interfere with her abilities to connect to other humans, it can make further traumatisation more likely.

The *trauma* victim becomes locked in a restrictive, double vicious circle, at the psychological and physical levels. The way she interprets relationships (her *inner working model*) can become distorted, so that she remains permanently watchful (*hyper-vigilant*) for, and unconsciously tends to bring about, further rejection or losses. The child may adopt patterns of interaction and attachment which are insecure, compliant, avoidant or ambivalent in an *adaptive* attempt to exert some control over her life. (Only very occasionally, under extremely damaging circumstances, will a child remain totally unattached and socially isolated.) In turn, any of these ways of interacting may make it more likely that the child's distorted beliefs about relationships are confirmed and that she is unlikely to achieve the depths of intimacy which would ultimately help to protect her and to heal her.

Simultaneously, the body's tendency to over-react can lead to full blown, *traumatic arousal* **in response to even minor, or benign** *triggers*, **which in turn reinforces her worst expectations and fears.** She may be easily startled, irritable, have difficulty focusing her attention and have sleep disturbances, including difficulty falling asleep and remaining asleep. She may lose the ability to discriminate between her feelings so that any excitement, positive or negative, can appear threatening. This phenomenon is known as *kindling* and can become generalised to include *stimuli* which bear little resemblance to the original overwhelming event. Thus her world becomes increasingly *constricted* and more rigid, as she struggles to avoid further hurts and to contain her terrors. These may also, apparently spontaneously, intrude into her consciousness during waking or sleep, as *flashbacks* or night terrors and repeated nightmares. She may then attempt to manage these internal feelings of stress by '*switching out*' (such as day dreaming or intense fantasy play) or '*switching off*', 'spacing out', 'blanking you off'. **These are forms of** *dissociation* **which are common responses to** *trauma*, **particularly where the** *trauma* **occurred very early on, or where the infant was simultaneously being exposed to drugs or alcohol.**

Dissociative responses begin as adaptive responses which can become unhealthy where they persist and are used repeatedly, since they lead to *avoidance* and *numbing* of feeling. In turn, this increases the likelihood that the child will go on believing the world to be a hostile and unpredictable place, as she may be unable to benefit from positive experience. *Kindling* (*traumatic* re-awakening of intense distress) and dissociation (lack of associations, including poor cognitive integration) are extremely important concepts, for **they can help us understand** *traumatised* **children's distorted responses and behaviour patterns and their seemingly stubborn resistance to change, despite alterations in circumstance.**

So when they come to us, traumatised children may go on behaving and reacting as if they are still being hurt or threatened or abused or abandoned: that is how it feels! **It is important that we validate the creativity, courage and endurance which has helped our youngsters to survive traumatic circumstances, even as we begin to encourage them to change.**

As new adoptive parents of babies and toddlers, all this may seem alarmist if not defeatist! You may have struggled for years to get to this point – to have a child of your own whom you so dearly wish to cherish and raise as if she were born to you. You may be thinking: 'Surely it can't be as bad as that? Surely all that stuff about bad blood and prejudice went out with the ark? Surely if I give a child enough time and love she will heal?'

Adoption is incontravertibly better for every child than leaving them in difficult circumstances, perhaps unwanted and unloved, potentially vulnerable to on-going abuse or neglect. It is difficult to think of anyone who would not agree that every child who comes into this world deserves a loving, stable home and the opportunity to thrive. That is why this book has been written!

If society cannot believe that adoptive parents have something to offer all children of whatever age, it might be better to campaign for the return of children's homes rather than for the better understanding of the needs of traumatised children and for better resources for adoptive families. However we, as adoptive parents, can only do the best for our children if we are alerted to the possible difficulties and prepared and supported to remedy them effectively. Knowledge is power. We can handle what we can understand and, in *developmental* terms, the sooner we start the better. In terms of *attachment*, too, sooner is also better. Since *attachment* involves reciprocal interaction and the development of *synchronic attunement* (which allow your little one to learn to regulate her rhythms and her arousal in tune with you), you stand a far better chance of bringing your youngster into healthy harmony with you and your family by starting right now. **Children who have not had the opportunity to learn to *modulate* their body's *arousal* early on may be so 'out of sync' that they throw your whole family 'out of sync' more readily than you are able to bring them down to your (relatively) functional and peaceful level.** (Please refer to Figure 4.4 on page 43.)

Remember, whilst potential for distortions of *attachment* and development may be greatest very early on, the potential for positive change is also greatest in those early years.

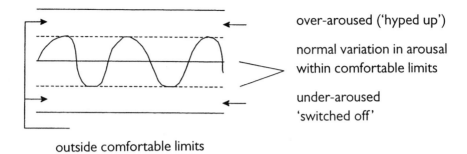

over-aroused ('hyped up')

normal variation in arousal within comfortable limits

under-aroused 'switched off'

outside comfortable limits

Figure 4.1 Normal pattern of arousal

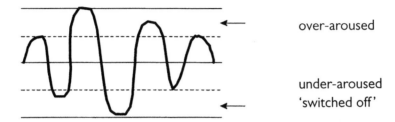

over-aroused

under-aroused 'switched off'

Figure 4.2 Pattern of extreme variation in the child who hurts

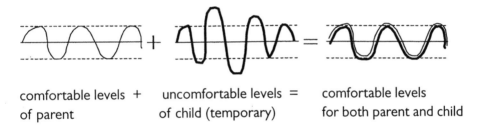

comfortable levels + uncomfortable levels = comfortable levels
of parent   of child (temporary)   for both parent and child

Figure 4.3 Using your own body rhythms to 'bring down' your child

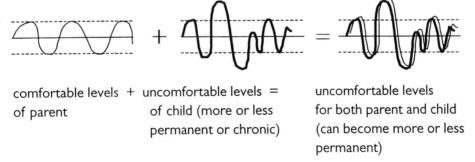

comfortable levels + uncomfortable levels = uncomfortable levels
of parent   of child (more or less   for both parent and child
                      permanent or chronic)   (can become more or less
                                                permanent)

Figure 4.4 What can happen in families with a child who hurts

Getting Back on Track

Encouraging Healthy Development in Babies and Young Children

Nurturing a baby or very young child is often exhausting and can become all-consuming. It is impossible to be with your little one twenty-four hours per day and stay sane, particularly if she is fussy or irritable. **Please try to make time just for yourself every day, in order to recharge your own batteries.** If you decide to follow some of the suggestions in this section, then do not set your expectations for yourself too high, or you may become emotionally drained. Why not work out what your ideal is and then think again! **Perhaps you could begin by trying out just one of the strategies for just a few minutes each day.** For the remainder of the day carry on as before. You will find that being realistic leaves you and your youngster feeling more positive and ready for more.

Below you will find suggestions for age and developmental stage appropriate activities which you and your child may enjoy, and which may have particular significance for infants and young children who have experienced *traumatic* losses and discontinuities in their early lives. They may also be very suitable, perhaps with some modification, for older children whose *developmental* age does not match up to their chronological age. For *traumatised* children this is very likely to be the case. It is hoped that these suggestions will offer you innovative, inspiring and exciting ways to reach the hurt child within.

The suggestions are grouped according to areas of special concern, although they all form part of an holistic process. They embrace ways of encouraging parent–child *attachment* relationships, emphasising the healthy give-and-take which is an essential part of your child's 'first year of life cycle', and the development of healthy *self-regulation*. Particular attention is paid, at the beginning, to eye contact and touch, since visual and tactile *awareness* constitute two of your infant's most vital early sensory pathways. Just as the eyes are often said to be 'the windows to the soul', so touch can be said to be the 'mother-tongue' through which our acceptance and loving feelings can be communicated. This is followed by discussion of some areas which may be of particular significance within adoptive families.

Here is a complete list of these sections with relevant page numbers:

Part Five

There may be times when you wish to concentrate solely on one sense, element of movement or attachment behaviour, and limit other potential distractions. At other times it may make more sense to incorporate several areas simultaneously. This can have the added advantage of allowing you to slip in a particularly sensitive piece of work alongside activities which your child may find more fun. It is also essential in encouraging *associations* between different areas of inner and outer experience and the processes of different levels of brain function.

If you can get a feel for where your little one is coming from, you stand a much better chance of joining him and leading him in the right direction. **At any one time the same child may display feelings, behaviours and levels of awareness, which indicate that you may be dealing with a functionally much younger child.** Matching your responses and interventions to his current, perhaps transient, developmental stage, using the same levels of intensity, will allow you to communicate on his wave-length and work towards bringing him into the here-and-now.

Begin by checking out for yourself where you are. Are you feeling warm, comfortable and at ease with yourself? Living with a little one who challenges your deepest beliefs about yourself as a reasonable human being may cause you to lose your sense of balance. It may help to spend time bringing yourself into the right frame of mind, the right spirit, to lead the way for your child. You may already have favourite ways of stepping back from a situation, such as counting slowly up to ten or taking a few deep breaths. Perhaps you could add to these ideas such activities as reading a special poem or short piece of prose, opening the window and looking at the flowers and trees, or taking a gentle walk around your garden. When you are more centred, 'coming from the right place', you are ready for action! (See also Part 5, section on 'Grounding'.)

You will find words in bold italics explained in the *Glossary* at the end of this book.

Encouraging Your Child's Sense of Self

Our *sense of self* is derived from becoming wholly aware of our bodies, and through building up ideas about ourselves in relation to, and separate from, others. Good nurturing experiences in the first years of life, a healthy balance between *stimulation* and *soothing*, the availability of consistent *attachment* figures who model self-care, and the safe opportunity to explore the environment all contribute to a sound *sense of self* in body and mind. For most of us, who have had a 'good enough' childhood, this will happen without us really having to think about it. For others, we may consciously have to go on working on our own sense of self throughout our life-times.

Little ones for whom these critical years do not go well will struggle to find themselves, to establish appropriate patterns of relating and comfortable *boundaries*, to acknowledge and respond to their own needs, feelings and emotions and to see themselves as powerful agents of their own destiny.

Throughout this book you will find suggestions which will address specific areas of your child's development at the physical, emotional, psychological, intellectual and spiritual levels. **These will all contribute to your child's ability to** *self-regulate,* **and to her** *self-awareness, self-esteem, self-confidence* **and** *self-respect.* We try to work 'upwards and outwards', in line with the upward and outward development of the brain and *neurological systems*. We begin with bodily *regulation* at the *brain stem* level, because that's where your baby begins. We then move on through attachment, arousal, *sensori-motor* experience and awareness of feelings, in the *mid brain* and *limbic system*, towards the beginnings of conscious awareness and an understanding of *self* at the thinking level.

One of the goals of the process is to get your little one to begin to be able to **think**, at that conscious level, to connect feeling and re-action through thought. **This is the part of the functioning puzzle which is often unavailable to children, and adults, who have been traumatised.** Furthermore, just as our thinking brain is made up of two halves, the left, logical, language-orientated side and the right, creative, intuitive side, we try to find a balance between reason and faith, order and spontaneity, verbal understanding and expressive activities.

It is hoped that all of the suggestions in this book will allow your child renewed opportunities to become *self-aware* in every dimension: to define who she is, where she is, what she can do and what she may be in thoughts and actions. Suggestions which begin by accepting and *reflecting back* your little one's expressions, movements and sounds will form a firm foundation on which you can build. In time you can draw her out into newer experiences of her *self*, and of you as uniquely separate beings, bound together by mutual love, acceptance and respect. **Please try to keep the over-riding concept of *self-awareness* in your minds as you walk through the growing process with your child.**

Encouraging Touch

Touch is an area which many children with *attachment* and *sensori-motor* difficulties find stressful or problematic. Some do not like the closeness and intimacy associated with touch, whilst others may be over-sensitive, especially to lighter forms of touch. **Children who have been abused may associate touch with the terror of being hurt. Where children have been neglected they may have turned within themselves for comfort and may not have learned the pleasures of touch.** Touch is one of the earliest forms of sensory awareness and it is essential that we provide our little ones with masses of opportunity to find out how good it can be, if they are to be at peace with the world.

Rather than trying to hold your little one close, it may be better to start by gently touching parts of her body, face, hands, feet and so on. Tickle your child gently, or gently tap or rub her face and neck. If your baby has problems tolerating lighter touch, try firmer (but still gentle) pressure instead. Frequently she will find this more comfortable and comforting. Research is showing that children with **autistic spectrum disorders** benefit more from the calming effects of **deep pressure** touch.

You could experiment with many different textures (such as lambskin, feather, silk, towelling) and patterns of stroking, tapping, patting, even licking. Find out which your child enjoys and work with those first. Gradually introduce the less favoured ones in her own time, perhaps coupled with ones she really likes.

If you feel comfortable with aromatherapy oils, giving your baby or young child a massage with one or two drops in a suitable carrier oil can be an excellent way to extend her sense of touch. If you choose a calming, relaxing oil for tense children, or possibly a mildly stimulating one for withdrawn children (clary sage, for example, can alter a tetchy child's mood), your child's experience of touch could be greatly enhanced. (See the Reading List at the back of the book for titles on baby massage and take a look in your bookshop or health food shop for further information on the healing properties of essential oils.)

Just taking a (shared) warm bath or bubble bath can be a simple and delightful way of enjoying touch. Add a few drops of an essential oil like lavender, chamomile or geranium and you will both become more relaxed in the process. Obviously, for little ones who are very sensitive to touch (*tactile sensory defensiveness*), you will need to introduce this very gradually. **For children who may have been sexually abused in the bath or bathroom, you will need to be aware of raised anxieties and of *triggering* a distress reaction.**

You will still want to introduce bathing as a pleasurable (though probably individual) experience as soon as you can. Perhaps you could start by giving dolly or teddy a bubble bath.

Both of you could help to wash and rub dolly or teddy dry, whilst putting names to body parts and even looking for your own. Then, of course, you can *model* cuddling and nurturing 'the baby' and begin to ask your child to help you.

Some children who have missed out on good touch attempt to fulfil this need for themselves: through rocking, head-banging, frantic sucking or hair twiddling. Children who have been sexually abused may try to engage others in sexual activity as the only way they know of attaining intimacy.

Others engage in *self-destructive* activities, such as picking, poking, bruising or cutting themselves (sometimes 'accidently'). Teenagers tend to gravitate towards self-medication, through for example, drinking, smoking, drug taking, or towards dangerous personal or sexual activities. These are all attempts to regulate stress levels (*arousal*), through *self-soothing*, or *self-stimulation*, which have their *physiological* roots in infant *trauma*.

You cannot easily stop your *hurt* child's (ineffective) attempts at *self-soothing*, or *self-stimulation*, so if you can't beat em, join 'em! Why not stroke your child's neck as she rocks or sucks, or run your fingers through her hair whilst humming quietly?

You could try rocking alongside her, slowing your rhythm gradually and bringing down her *arousal*, or stroking or tickling her tummy. This way you are emphasising that your child does not have to *soothe* or *stimulate* herself, and that getting close is more comforting or rewarding. (You may also find time to relax too, especially if you surround yourselves with blankets and pillows and put on a tape of calming music.)

As you join your child, you can gradually begin to reduce the unwanted activity and replace it with a more acceptable one. **Only after your child has learned to accept comfort or pleasure from you will she begin to learn to comfort or please herself.** Very *hurt*, and much older children may need more specific help to let go of old survival patterns.

Blowing bubbles and allowing your child to reach out to touch them is a wonderful way of encouraging him to relate through his fingers and his eyes. You can begin by introducing your baby to the magic of bubbles floating in the air and landing on his skin when he is just a few months old. Don't forget to name the body parts as the bubbles land! Try sitting directly across from your youngster (but beware of blowing soap into his eyes), so that you are engaging his attention and his eyes.

Gradually your toddler can learn to dip the wand into the sticky soap liquid and create magic bubbles for himself. Take turns blowing and watching the bubble spheres float into the air. Catching them together is great fun too!

As your child gets older, you can extend this to blowing paint or soap. Use long straws (the curly see-through ones are great for this) and blow paint on paper to make your own unique pictures. Have a straw each and share the pool of paint for closer encounters, where you 'accidently' rub against his shoulder, his arm, his knee. Later you can enthusiastically display the resulting works of art in an appropriate place and allow your child to finger and talk about his achievement with pride!

Cleaning up any mess can also encourage joint activity and acceptance of legitimate touch, for example foot painting will leave you with the perfect excuse to carry your child to the kitchen or bathroom to wash his feet.

Painting your child's face, hands or feet with face paints or plain water can be great fun, with great opportunities for closeness, touch, talking about bodies and another chance to wash together when it's all over (the carpet?). Add grainy materials for extra texture. **Be aware of possible *triggers* for children who may have been abused or where cleanliness or physical care have been grossly neglected.**

Put lentils, dried beans, rice and pasta shapes in boxes and hide small objects within. Ask your child to feel inside to find them. As he pulls the objects out, tell him what he is doing, or name them together. Later on your child can begin to guess what the 'surprise' is before he pulls it out.

You could also try blowing feathers, balloons or tissue paper. If your child tends to be destructive, ask him to tear up lots of paper first so that you can both blow it at each other. Of course he will be expected to join in the clearing up afterwards. It is never too early to start practising the sharing of little chores!

Some small children (and larger ones) are highly sensitive to touch around or in their mouths. **Having the bottle rammed into the baby's mouth, being fed roughly or carelessly, or being orally abused may be responsible for this. You will have to go very slowly and carefully here.** Try tapping gently around the edges of the lips and over the cheeks and chin with your finger (or a feather) for a few minutes each day to make the mouth area less sensitive.

Sucking or blowing through straws can also help with *oral sensitivity* and developing muscle control. This could be useful if your little one dribbles excessively or tends to keep his mouth open all the time. Very chewy items of food such as toffee and chewing gum (in time!) can also supply *deep pressure* experiences within the mouth.

Put honey around the child's lips and ask him to lick it off, or join in the licking yourself if you think he could tolerate this. Try using chocolate spread or even marmite instead.

Make real mud pies with your child. Or bake 'mud pie' cakes (you can buy ready-to-use kits!) and don't stint on the shared mixing, tasting and finger licking or on the water and bubbles for the washing up.

Share a sticky bun, starting from opposite ends and finishing nose to nose. Or feed each other, the messier the better. You can introduce different textures and tastes (and smells) of food as you go. **Be watchful for any tastes, smells or textures which *trigger* distress, especially if your child has been orally abused or has been deprived of a normal range of food experience.**

For youngsters who react badly to the wind on their faces, or in their hair, it is important to take things slowly. Can your child tolerate you blowing gently down his neck or on his arm, hand or leg? Build up the 'wind' strength and the area exposed as your child becomes used to these sensations. Show him how much fun you can have with a stiff breeze in your hair. **Hair driers and fans may not be a good idea, because they are too powerful and very noisy.**

Children with sluggish reactions, *over-compliant* and '*switched off*' (*avoidant*) children may respond to unexpected blasts of air down their necks or up their trouser legs!

Remember, it is the element of surprise, combined with a shared sense of fun, which is important here. **Please beware of startling or distressing your child**, since if you unwittingly *kindle* (*trigger*) a fear or distress response your child may become more '*switched off*' or '*spaced out*' and you will be unwittingly reinforcing her *dissociative response.*

Try 'belly-blobbing', a game to help more mobile, sturdier toddlers and older children to enjoy touch. Tie cushions round each of you, put some more cushions on the floor and enjoy the rough and tumble of bumping into each other!

Arrange an obstacle course with a tunnel for your child to crawl through. This is another fun way to help her to become used to banging into things. **Be sensitive to little ones who have a fear of the dark or of confined spaces.**

Make a 'child sandwich' using two duvets or eiderdowns for the bread. Gently squash your child in the middle and have extra fun stuffing in appropriate 'tomatoes', 'mayonnaise', 'crisps' and so on to spice up the game. The *deep pressure* your child will experience (especially if you press down the top 'slice') may be more acceptable and healing than skin-deep touch. **Again, be aware of any history of abuse or maltreatment here.** In this case, perhaps your child would like to make *you* into a sandwich instead. You could then gradually begin to swap roles (rolls!).

Water and Sand Play
(More Ideas for Encouraging Touch)

Water play can be a great stand-by to develop the experience of touch. From face-to-face over the washing up bowl to learning to swim in the swimming pool or sea, there is always an excuse for extra close encounters.

Hose pipes, watering cans, water pistols or even old washing up liquid containers can add to your fun!

For children who are over-sensitive to water, you will have to go gently. Does your child like watching fountains or streams flowing over rocks and under bridges? Can he gradually be encouraged to dip his fingertips or toes into the flow? How would he respond if you suddenly started dancing in the fountain or wading in the stream – and how would you feel?

How about a foot bath in your kitchen bowl using bubbly water: do you have a foot spa? Or why not bath the dog together?

Watching raindrops run down the window can lead to poking noses or fingers out into the wet – especially if you take the lead in this.

Take your child out into the rain and encourage her to jump in the puddles. Wellies and rainsuits provide suitable protection (plus brolly for the full effect) as your child gets used to the rain outside. Maybe she could even enjoy streaking in the rain on a warmer day! **This may not be suitable initially where a child has been exposed to sexual abuse, has been made to feel shameful about her own body, or has not learned the social rules around nakedness.**

What about practising dancing in the rain to an appropriate tune? *Singing in the Rain* springs immediately to mind. Ignore the neighbours and concentrate on having fun.

For *avoidant* or *over-compliant* children, try creeping up and squirting them when they least expect it. Fall about laughing, to *model* an appropriate response and then let her do the same to you. Be sure to laugh *with* her and not *at* her, and be **sensitive to little ones who may respond by further withdrawal.**

Sand play, when you can bear the mess, is another way to encourage touching and feeling. Keep the sand box small, sit facing each other and you will be promoting mutual interaction and eye contact simultaneously. Make it big (or get down onto the beach) and you can both have an all-body experience! Remember the benefits of having to take responsibility for cleaning up your child at the end of the game, either way.

There are lots of games you can play using sand which can involve you both in close, fun activities. **Some children may show clear distress at 'getting messy' or dislike the 'feel' of the sand. Take your time and avoid undue pressure.** Gradually you may be able to bring your child round and start to enjoy 'messiness' together.

Try hiding small toys and play at hunting for them in the sand. Name them as they are found. You can express surprise and delight when you 'find' your child's fingers rather than the toy.

Your play can extend to include imaginary deserts and deserted islands as your little one matures. **Be aware that for your child being 'cast away' or feeling abandoned in a deserted place, may have been a reality for her.** Introduce this idea gradually as you play and allow your child to explore her feelings while she is busy. She may be more able to talk about these feelings within this context than facing them directly.

Encouraging Eye Contact and Visual Perception

There are many brightly coloured cot and pram toys and mobiles available which will catch your baby's eye. They will become even more interesting if they are accompanied by movement and sound and by your presence. **Remember that the best visual *stimuli* are your face, your eyes and your smile.** Within weeks of birth, babies actively respond to representations of the human face in preference to other *stimuli*.

Try to find as many 'natural' opportunities as you can to look into your little one's eyes. This is especially beneficial when you are holding her or feeding her, since you will be connecting through several different sensory paths at the same time. **But please be aware of communicating anxiety and of the baby's need to look away at times.** (See also Part 3: When Things Don't Seem Quite Right, page 32 'gaze avert'.)

Take your time in encouraging eye contact where your child shows distress but keep at the back of your mind that making connection through your eyes is an essential ultimate goal.

'Peek-a Boo' is an excellent, fun way to encourage eye contact and can be done from the early months of your child's life. As it alternates with looking away (*gaze avert*), it is has built-in *arousal* safety measures!

'Peek-a-Boo' can be extended to simple hide-and-seek games as your child matures. These reinforce a sense of *object constancy* (e.g. if you hide, you can quickly be found again and are not lost forever) and allow your little one to practise moving away from you briefly, when it is her turn to hide. **For children who may have been left alone for long periods, approach this one with particular caution.**

As your child is increasingly able to join in by hiding herself, she will begin to develop an awareness of space and *boundaries* (me and not me), a sense of *self-identity* and *self-constancy*. A young child can also be helped to feel in control of herself (*self-competence*) and can be reassured that you will always come and find her. Do not forget to go over the top with surprise and delight when you do!

'Squeak Piggy Squeak' and 'Sardines' are interesting variations of this game. **Please be aware of your little one's early history. If your child was neglected, the shortest separations may be stressful. If she was abused, the sense of intimacy combined with secrecy in these games could be very distressing to her. Take your time.**

Games with torchlight under the table, or behind the sofa can also be fun. Try throwing shadows of your child onto a plain (or patterned!) wall, or lighting only part of a familiar toy and encourage her to guess what it is. **As always, be sensitive to your child's possible fear of the dark and of shadowy figures.** It may take time and gentle encouragement before she can enjoy such games.

Nursery rhymes with hand and facial movements, such as 'Two Little Dicky Birds', and 'Little Peter Rabbit', or accompanied by simple finger puppets, will add to your visual repertoire as your child grows.

Using regular *holding time* can give you many additional, excellent opportunities for making eye contact safely (see Section on **Safe Holding**, page 69).

Encouraging Awareness of Movement

Movement is vitally important to all developing human beings. Premature babies miss out on essential movement in the womb and have been shown to benefit from extra rocking, which provides additional opportunities to learn about body position (***proprioception***), balance and spatial awareness (***vestibular stimulation***). So, too, might your little one, or those bigger ones who seem 'clumsy' (***dyspraxic***).

Gentle rocking in your arms is by far the best starting point, perhaps as you walk around the room slowly, singing lullabies or nursery rhymes.

A rocking chair can be really useful for young children who need this sort of experience, since by sharing this time you will be providing a ***containing***, warm, and rhythmic environment. This can be very comforting, as it both re-creates the experience in the womb, and allows your infant to learn how to ***self-soothe***. In this context you can gradually introduce stroking, cuddling and hugging as well as rhythmic nursery songs such as 'Rock a Bye Baby'. **Some children who use rocking in attempts to** *self-soothe* **may especially need your help – to begin to associate comfort with close contact as well as rocking movement.** (See also Part 4.)

The carrying slings, referred to in Part 1, are another very good way to accustom your baby to gentle movement. You can also use the closeness they provide to help your child tune in to your internal body rhythms and movements, thus encouraging ***self-regulation*** through your own example (***modelling***).

As your child grows older, baby swings, rocking horses and see-saws (especially the human kind) all mirror the rocking movement, which hopefully he will have learned to enjoy. Older ones who may have missed out on early movement will also benefit from being able to play in this way. Later you can sit together on a good-sized swing, enjoying both the movement and the closeness.

Trips in the pushchair, in the car or on boats on the park lake can all add to the wealth of experience of movement as your little one grows, **but be aware of anxieties about travel/moving** (see Part 1). Don't forget to point out how things around him may change as he moves in relation to them.

Toddlers and upward may like to share a small trampoline with you, before moving on to bouncing by themselves here, on big bouncy balls or even bouncing castles. Where you can't physically join them, why not stand close by and clap or sing to the rhythm of your child's jumping? **Some children may find this too stressful at first – that's O.K., just take it very slowly.**

You can increase your opportunities for body movement and *spatial awareness* by setting aside regular (or spontaneous) times for singing, dancing and action songs. Try 'Horsey, Horsey', 'Hokey Cokey', 'The Wheels on the Bus' and all the others you can think of! What are your favourites?

Swinging garden seats and hammocks can also give you extra chances at closeness, with the added fun of swinging, as your child grows. Have you tried 'Swinging in the Rain'?

Go along to your local park and join in the fun on swings, roundabouts, see-saws, slides and anything else that moves. **Do take it easy if your child has difficulties with too much excitement or noise.**

For much older ones, the fun fair could provide the perfect excuse you need, as long as you can stand the pace yourself! **Try to build in some natural relaxation once it's all over.**

Encouraging Children to Know Their Own Bodies

Some children do not have a good sense of their own bodies or their own physical needs, particularly if their first few months have been disturbed. If there was an inconsistent response to the infant's needs, or inadequate *mirroring* of his early attempts at *self-expression*, he may not learn to recognise his internal body messages. The connections between body and mind remain weak. Similarly if he meets criticism, denial, abuse, pain or neglect, he may learn to switch off from recognising his own responses in order to survive. Unless your child can begin to *associate* these body sensations and feelings with his responses, he will remain prone to *impulsivity* and potentially *self-harming* behaviours.

Be a human mirror: reflecting back to your little one an exaggerated image of himself. He will then begin to see himself through your eyes. Gradually introduce the naming of his expressions and body parts and your interpretations of them. Make **statements** about what he is doing rather than asking questions. Include feelings, both 'good' and 'bad', as your child matures. You will be establishing essential *neurological connections* and *associations* between different aspects of your child's body, behaviour, emotions, *sensori-motor* experience and understanding.

Why not begin early on with a mirror and labour the point about whose face you can both see? As the child grows, get a bigger mirror and include his whole body! Continue to give names to all his body parts. You could include rhymes, such as 'Heads, Shoulder, Knees and Toes' and 'One Finger, One Thumb Keep Moving', to add to the fun.

Don't forget the age-old tradition of marking off your child's height against the bedroom door, alongside other members of your family. That will give him a concrete idea of himself and show him how you are all changing over time.

Toddlers can enjoy lying on paper whilst you cut round their whole body, or parts such as head, hands and feet. **Be aware of *triggering* a fear reaction if knives or scissors are associated with your child's early experiences of maltreatment, witnessing violence, or abuse.**

Wet sand can be used for body prints or part-body prints. Your more mobile child may enjoy 'action replays' of himself jumping, lying on his back making 'angels in the snow', or 'bouncing-bottom' prints too.

You could even make plaster of Paris moulds of your youngster and keep them for (posterior) posterity!

You could take a leaf out of Archimedes' book, and fill up a bath tub outside in the sunshine. Ask your little one to get into the warm water **(unless he has specific problems with water)** and watch the water overflow! You could colour the water for added effect. The more enterprising, or more scientific, of you could find ways of measuring mass and volume before and after immersion, to work out your child's weight and volume.

A large, inflatable ball upon which your youngster may balance, and perhaps roll, may help him develop a sense of his body in space, and increase global *spatial awareness*. Try it lying on his back and on his front. You could introduce easy instructions, such as 'raise one leg' (and do it with him) as he matures. **Take it very slowly here, if your child shows any distress.**

'Pat-a-Cake' and every other hand and finger game you can think of, such as 'Round and Round the Garden' and 'This Little Piggy', can establish permissible, fun touch which also develops a sense of body awareness and rhythm. Why not obtain a copy of an excellent paperback of children's rhymes called *This Little Puffin*, for added inspiration? Here you are beginning to help your child to differentiate between parts of his own body and between his body and yours. This is the beginning of awareness of difference and **boundaries** between self and others, which is essential for true *self-consciousness* and *self-awareness*.

With older, school-age kids, this can be extended to games and hand clapping rhymes such as 'My Mother Told Me'.

Try also cat's cradle games for encouraging dexterity and test your own memories and co-ordination at the same time! You may also be able to sneak in some extra eye and hand contact in the course of the game. **Take care if you suspect that rope, string or other means of tying up were used in the abuse of your child.**

Prone Position Activities
(More Ideas for Encouraging Children to Know Their Own Bodies)

The *prone* position is developmentally important for your infant to gain posture and motor control and to strengthen balance. He should begin to arch his back and raise both head and feet from the ground at around four to six months of age. Gentle encouragement, with lots of eye contact and *physical prompts,* should help your child to develop these skills. However you will have to get right down there with him to stay in touch.

As your youngster develops, he should be able to begin moving towards you, or towards his other favourite toys. Your eye contact and verbal encouragement should help him to feel safe enough to do this.

Try rolling your toddler, lying on his tummy, on a skateboard, **as soon as this feels right to you**. Rolling down very gentle grassy inclines (with or without the board) can be great fun too and again will encourage the arching back, while the inevitable bumps and tumbles encourage his awareness of his body.

Try it yourself, or give him a 'piggy back on wheels'! When you fall off, roll over and hug him as if you are 'saving' him. Then do it all over again.

Ordinary piggy back and horsey rides are also good for close encounters with baby's own and other people's bodies, and they are good fun. You could ride an obstacle course of cardboard boxes or through a bunch of free-floating balloons, or even through water or mud. **Proceed with caution with this one, where you believe there has been sexual or physical abuse or you see indications of distress.**

For the little (and bigger) ones who do not do well at making their needs known by asking, you could try requiring directions for the 'horse'. This can allow important repair work while you both have fun, since the 'horse' will be too stupid to know the right way like your child does! (See also section on Encouraging Children Who Seem too Afraid to Ask for What they Need.)

Older ones may enjoy 'tummy-tug-of-war', where you each sit or lie on a firm surface scattered with cushions and try to pull each other into the 'sea' (a rolled up towel) between you. **Again, if you sense that this triggers memories of witnessed violence, approach this one with caution.**

Encouraging Awareness of Sound

A baby will respond to gentle, soothing, soft sounds, which re-create the heartbeat she has been picking up in the womb, by becoming more relaxed in body and mind. As you hold her close to you, she will begin to pick up on your heart rhythm and relax into you. We have always known that singing lullabies and humming simple, rhythmic melodies, or even the repetitive ticking of a clock, can help calm a tense or crying infant. Once these *associations* between rhythmic sounds and soothing are established we can continue to use them as the child grows.

Babies who have been been used to having their peace broken by sudden, loud noises or angry voices (even before they were born) may be particularly sensitive to sound and easily aroused by everyday levels of background noise. They may remain ever watchful (*hyper-vigilant*) for the next flood of sound. Others may have become so used to the hubbub of a busy nursery, for example, that they become anxious if things are too quiet. **These little ones may need special nurturing and extra opportunities to begin to make sense of their world and to heal.**

Talk to your child in a gentle, soothing way. You can do this even while you are doing something else, reassuring your baby that you are still there, even if she cannot see you.

The latest in 'sound and light' gadgets for babies could be very useful. Your child does not need to be a baby to enjoy the calming lullabies and soft, moving lights. Pour yourself a cup of tea (Earl Grey can be especially good for calming!) and enjoy this quiet time too.

At more alert times, try tying a small set of bells around his wrist or ankle. You can buy ready-made bell strips, or make your own using broad ribbon. Your very young child will be fascinated by his own ability to generate sounds. For slightly older infants this can help them to become more aware of their own bodies and their movements. Putting names to your child's activities and limbs adds to his experience of learning about *self.*

Humming tops and musical boxes are still around and can provide great fun! Try all these sorts of things out before you buy them. You might even persuade your local toy shop to let you take things home on trial, if you explain your child's difficulties. Toy libraries may have just the thing you need – although primarily catering for children with recognisable disabilities, there is no reason why you couldn't try to persuade them to let you borrow toys and equipment too.

Simple, rhythmic clapping songs, such as 'If you're Happy and You Know It' and 'Roll The Bobbin' can be fun ways to become more familiar with sound. Begin with the child on your knee, facing you when she is very little, and take it from there.

Extend this by clapping or tapping out rhythms and taking turns to repeat the short sequences. Or use your whole body to bounce out a rhythm! **Take extra care if your child has been violently shaken or abused.**

Find ways of making sounds which she can feel as well as hear. You can talk about where she feels the sound vibrations in her body. Do you have a tuning fork in the house?

Get hold of a toy stethoscope and allow your child to hear her own heart sounds, and yours. The connection with the heart is a very special one and you can use this opportunity, in time, to talk about separations and *hurts* and making new connections.

There are several 'sound lotto' games on the market which you and your toddler (and upwards) can enjoy together. This can also be the beginning of learning to take turns, another great opportunity for mutual responses, eye contact, *physical prompts* and essential 'me and not me' experiences.

See if your little one responds better to low notes or high notes, quick ones or slow ones. Does she show a preference for classics, pops or ballads, folk or tribal music? Try them all! Music has many cultural overtones and you can begin to introduce ideas of belonging, community and ethnicity as you play.

Practise loud action songs and exaggerate these using words, facial expressions and actions. **Be aware that you could over-stimulate a sensitive little one.** Remember you can always bring him back with some quiet songs to close.

Extend your use of sounds to introduce a range of feelings, beginning with mad (angry, not crazy), sad, glad and scared. You can make a good sound on drums (or pots and pans) to express how you think your little one is feeling. If you can get her to join in, so much the better, but don't worry if you play solo! You can use this to try to get her to acknowledge anger and sadness, which

she may be trying to push away. You can show her (through **modelling**) that it is safe to let out her feelings by stamping loudly, crashing tin lids, singing at the top of her voice.

Water makes wonderful sounds. It can be poured, splashed in, tinkled into a glass, gurgled down a throat. Don't forget the natural sounds of water running down a mountain, roaring in a waterfall, crashing onto rocks, lapping against the shore. These are amazing experiences and great opportunities to begin to tune your youngster in to the wonders of nature.

You can select 'feelings' music for the kitchen, the living room, the car, the bedroom, to **modulate** your child's activity and **arousal** levels. Mozart can work well for calming. The Rolling Stones can raise the roof and lift the lid, if and when you choose! 'Switched off', **avoidant** children may need this sort of stimulus to get in touch, but **steer clear of startling sounds or threatening music.**

Encouraging Awareness of Smell

Our sense of smell is more important than we think! Not only does it keep us safe, by alerting us to rotting foods and contaminated water for example, but it also forms the most powerful connection to our memories and our emotions. Think of the smells which elicit emotional responses in your own life – they can transport you back to happy and unhappy times in a flash. The odours we inhale go directly to our organs of smell (the **olfactory bulbs**) within the **limbic system** of our brain, arousing our awareness more or less instantaneously.

Ensure you do not eliminate the good (for him) smells your child brings with him. Allow him to keep familiar toys, 'blankies', and so on unwashed, however unhygienic you think they are. They are pungent, comforting reminders of the past.

Try to use the same washing powders and softeners as his previous family, at least until he has absorbed some of the odours of your home.

Remember that some children become so used to the smell of urine, that they continue to wet themselves, and their beds, to re-create that old, familiar situation – even if there are many painful *associations* too.

Other children may have very confused and confusing responses to the smells of 'wee' and 'poo'. If they have been criticised or punished for wetting or soiling themselves in the past, they may associate such smells with being bad and/or dirty. This may make them more concerned about cleanliness or, conversely, more likely to go on 'making a mess', as a metaphor for how they see themselves. **Watch out for any smells which *trigger* difficult feelings or behaviours.**

Be very careful to avoid showing your frustration, annoyance or disgust if your child continues to wet or soil, particularly if he seems not to care. Making an issue out of what is essentially a natural and necessary function can increase problems and may re-create the punitive or abusive responses which were experienced in the birth family.

We can use different pleasant aromas to arouse our sense of smell, and in turn heighten our other senses. For very young children, smell is likely to be their most heightened sense – use it to communicate as much as you can.

Show your young child how to sniff things and watch which smells give her pleasure. Use everyday things you find in your kitchen, your bathroom, your garden. **Watch out also for nose-rubbing, eye watering, sneezing or dis-smell – the intense dislike of an odour.** These could be indicators of particular sensitivities, or past *hurtful* experiences which you may want to avoid, to begin with at least.

Taste is predominantly an extension of the sense of smell, so why not include tasting games too? Provide a wide range of textures, smooth, thick, runny, lumpy, coarse. **Do be aware of any which cause disgust (literally, the taste equivalent of dis-smell) to your child: this may be due to earlier frightening or painful experiences, including oral sexual abuse.**

Play sniffing games, using blindfolds or concealing 'smelly' objects under cloths or in boxes. 'Fee, Fi, Fo, Fum' (without the old, racist 'Englishman' line) can be a good way of practising guessing who has just been in the room. Some children have a really sensitive sense of smell and can pick up Auntie Dot's hairspray at six miles! They could be your 'smell detectives', 'sniffing out clues' or 'smelling a rat'.

Get hold of some of those (irritating) 'scratch and sniff' books and even some 'smelly' pens if you can bear them! You can always open the windows later! **Some children may become 'hyped up' by some of the chemicals in felt pens, so take care!**

Take your more mobile ones outside and get them smelling the flowers, the leaves, the rain, the wind, even the snow and the fog. Draw their attention to tar smells on hot days, burning wood (somebody else's preferably), buses, trains, hot dog sellers and so on.

Baking bread, cakes, potatoes or even fish fingers can bring more smells into your conversation. Later on, introduce baby smells and talk about your child's early life story together.

You may like to familiarise yourself with essential oils, the concentrated essences of flowers, plants and trees which have been painstakingly distilled. We all know how uplifting these fragrances can be in the wild (and in the garden); it could just be that they are equally, or more, powerful when concentrated in this way. There are so many aromatherapy oils now available, and each is said to have its own particular fragrance, healing properties and meaning. You could use them for yourself and for your whole family, in burners, in a bowl of warm water, in the bath, or in massage oils, depending on your mood. **Since the aromas go directly to the same areas of the brain which handle emotions and *arousal*, this can be a particularly pleasant and easy way of re-balancing yourself and your child.**

Grounding (Bringing Down to Earth)

No, this is not, as you might expect, the 'you are grounded for a week' as punishment routine. **It is vital that you always try to avoid punishment,** since this teaches only revenge, doesn't allow a child to begin to *associate* causes and effects of their own behaviours, can *kindle* a rage or fear reaction, or *reinforce withdrawal* or *avoidance* by the child. In any case that sort of grounding is hard to keep up and isn't much fun, especially for the grounder! The occasional *time out* may be fine, but 'time in' spent close to you may be far more effective.

Real grounding is about bringing down to earth gently. Children who tend to be *impulsive, hyperactive*, irritable or excitable on the one hand, or 'in a dream world', '*switched off*', overly subdued or unexpressive on the other, are unable to find a comfortable balance in their bodies and feelings. They need your help to manage their inner chaos or *numbness* or fogging. (See arousal diagrams on page 43.)

Begin by following some of the suggestions in the sensory sections above, such as touch, sound, smell and movement, which are designed to develop *self-regulation* and *self-awareness*. Gradually you should see changes for the better and you may not need to do anything more. For other little ones, and bigger ones who haven't had the benefit of the early strategies, you may wish to supplement your energies and ideas from the suggestions which follow.

You should begin by practising grounding yourself. One of the easiest ways is to stand, or sit, with both feet firmly planted on the ground and take some slow, deep breaths. Connect your in-breath to your out-breath, breathing into your belly and emphasising your out-breath in one slow, continuous movement. Taking off your shoes and socks and standing ankle deep in wet grass in the park can have a similar effect, by allowing you to tune into the harmonising rhythms of the natural world. If you feel the urge, run! This can allow us to 'move on' when our energies are stuck. Why not be adventurous and try a few Yoga, Reiki, Shiatsu or Tai Chi exercises or Cook's Hook Ups (Brain Gym)?

Use this time of peace to re-affirm your belief in yourself and your ability to get through. You may need to 'go over the top' with this for just a little while, until your confidence returns. Although it may seem silly or embarrassing, it really is vital that you feel sure of yourself and what you are doing, especially when you are trying to take care of a child for whom *un*certainty has been so painfully familiar. Affirmations such as 'I have everything I need', 'I approve of myself' or 'I accept myself as I am' can be used at this, and other times. Write them down and stick them on the fridge door, or shout them out loud in the bath, or to the stars. This has to be a case of 'physician heal thyself' first. You are then in a better position to help your **hurt** child.

One of the best ways of grounding a small child is by simply laying your hand on his arm and bringing him into your body. You are effectively 'earthing' him. **Be sure to do this slowly and gently, to avoid *triggers* of past *hurts*.**

Some young children may seem so distressed that spontaneous *holding time* is called for (see section on 'Safe Holding'.) Because in this form of *holding* for nurture you gently cradle the child in the position of a new-born, and provide the safe *containment* for his greatest fears, you allow him to re-connect with you and experience, perhaps for the first time, the powerful healing of touch. Slowly his breathing, heart rate and body temperature will adjust to yours and he will feel a greater sense of well-being. **Although your youngster may well resist being held at first, he will gradually learn the comforts of being securely held, if you remain patient and sympathetic to his initial distress.**

These changes in his body can occur alongside more gradual, more permanent, alterations to his perceptions of the world as hostile, chaotic and terrifying and of himself as untouchable, unlovable and out of control. Whether your child is 'over the top' or appears 'not to be here', this gentle approach can bring him to a more comfortable place and help him feel more 'real' and more alive.

If your little one seems too threatened by such close contact, you could begin by wrapping him in a soft blanket or sheet (see also section on 'Crying Babies'). This may give him a sense of secure containment without feeling invaded. **Stay vigilant for children who may have had experiences of neglect or abuse which could be *triggered* in this way.**

Making contact through the eyes can also be grounding for your youngster. Looking into each other's eyes, 'the windows to the soul', is connecting at a very deep level and can bring a child who has 'shut you out' or 'shut off' (*dissociated*) back into reality.

Of course there are many possible reasons why your child may seem *impulsive*, have poor attention span and appear over-active. *Attention Deficit Disorder* (*ADD*) and *Attention Deficit Hyperactivity Disorder (ADHD)* may have a genetic component, that is the predisposition for these behaviours may already be established. **However, that doesn't mean that you can't do your best to minimise its likelihood or its effects.** Recent research has shown that one of the causes of such problems is the effect of very early *trauma* on the *neuro-physiology* and *bio-chemistry* of the developing infant. (See Part 4 .)

Hence ready distractibility, impulsivity and *hyperkinesis* (over-activity) can frequently be linked to early adversity and may be perceived, in part, as *functional* responses to abnormal experience. The child's ability to learn from subsequent experience may be compromised and he may need repeated *soothing* interactions, (such as *holding*), to re-learn healthier patterns of responding to his social and physical world.

Under-responsiveness and *withdrawal* are also common reactions to *trauma*. For youngsters who have experienced neglectful or grossly inconsistent care, they may never have made any meaningful connections with others and may have retreated into their own world, created within their own heads. Overwhelming experience of fear or pain, through medical interventions, abuse, losses or natural disaster, may also lead to the shattering of those connections and with any existing sense of *self*. **The child is then forced to live his life as if he is totally alone and to try to avoid any situation which may *re-kindle* his overwhelming sense of terror and emptiness.**

Since the pain and fear is most often connected to human action or inaction, your young child may do his best to stay 'safe' by distancing himself from others, and from his own needs and feelings. Your touch and your eye contact can bring him back to earth.

Stimulating physical activity, such as running full tilt, can also help to 'change where he is'. This is particularly important for little ones who have experienced *trauma* when they were too young and helpless to respond by *'fight or flight'* at the time. At a deep physical level you can begin to free up your child's body and help him to feel more powerful, both physically and *psychologically*.

For these youngsters, we have to find ways to get in touch which do not cause them to retreat further into themselves, which is a difficult enough task in itself. It is sometimes made more difficult because your child's inner defences may activate feelings within you, such as frustration, rejection and rage as well as intense sadness, which can get in the way of your ability to be patient, accepting, loving and warm.

That is why strategies such as taking care of yourself, grounding, affirming, setting boundaries and having time to yourself are all so vital. And that is why getting in touch with your child through *holding*, eye contact and shared closeness are so essential for your child, since they will help her get in touch with herself and begin to learn to *regulate* her body, her feelings and her world.

You will also need to choose patterns of engaging with your child which, without overwhelming the child, offer elements of surprise, novelty and fun, and which are sufficiently intense and pleasurable to reach her. These are the things which are most likely to grab her attention and gradually draw her out of her isolation and into life. (See also section on 'Encouraging Children to Know and Show Their Feelings'.)

Safe Holding (Holding Time)

You will naturally be creating as many opportunities as you can to hold your child, throughout the day. However, for some children this just doesn't seem enough, and it may then be time to set up planned *holding times*, during which you and your child can be physically close *and* have the chance to share anything and everything you are both feeling, whether it is laughter or sadness, joy or anger.

Parent–child *holding time* is a very safe and caring way to get close to your child, to help him to learn to manage his body and his feelings and to begin to heal some of his early *hurts*. It can enable you to 'claim' your young child as your own and provide the secure *containment* which he so desperately needs, and yet so often fights against. You will be hoping to let your young child sense all these things in the cuddles you give, the games you play, the stories you read, the smiles and tears you share, throughout the course of your day. *Holding* is just a particularly powerful way of getting your messages across, in a way which can be taken in and comprehended by a hurt child.

Accounts from adult adoptees and from adoptive parents show that despite *good enough* parenting (see Part 1: Coming Home), the adopted child or adult frequently continues to feel different, as though they don't belong, are unwanted or untouchable. *Holding* can give you an extra dimension in your relationship which can help you break through and reach greater intimacy and connectedness with your youngster, right from the start. During *holding* you can express your own sadness for, and anger about, the *hurts* which your child has experienced in his body and his soul. Whilst your words can take him so far along the road to *self-awareness*, your touch and your physical closeness can take him several steps closer.

Holding can ground your child, bring him close enough to begin to regulate his levels of distress, and show him that you are in control, can handle his anger and can still be there for him. It lets him know, through non-verbal channels, that he is not alone and that all parts of him, his 'good' behaviours and his 'bad' ones are acceptable and manageable at a time when he is 'lost for words'.

Holding time is a very personal thing and, if you are thinking of using it with your child, you will need to take your time to find out as much as you can before you begin. Talk to other parents who are familiar with *holding* and share your hopes and fears with them. (You could use the Experience Resource Bank (ERBIE) at Adoption UK to make contact with other families familiar with holding.)

It is essential that you feel totally comfortable and confident before you use *holding*, not least because your child will be able to pick up on any doubts you have and will not then derive the sense of security from the experience which he needs. Only you can make the decision to use *holding* with your child: that this is the right thing to do and the right time to do it. It is a very emotionally draining process – although it certainly can be very rewarding for all of you.

(Specific suggestions for the use of holding, and the rationale behind it, are contained in papers available from Adoption UK. The book *Holding Time*, by Martha Welch, an American paediatrician, also contains a great deal of helpful information and advice (see Reading List).)

Crying Babies

Some babies do cry a lot and babies who have experienced separations, unpredictability and very early life *traumas* often express their distress in this way. Others may stay silent and unheard. It may be difficult for you to help your baby through this time, especially if she goes through repeated bouts of excessive crying or screaming. Her anxiety will tend to make you feel tense and anxious too. That is *adaptive*, since nature intended us to respond to a helpless baby right away (and gave the baby a good pair of lungs to help let us know!) However, in this time of small, nuclear families, and (predominantly male) 'experts' who tell us what to do and how to do it, it is harder for us to trust our instincts and have the confidence that we know what we are doing. **Try to listen to your own heart**, rather than to outsiders – however well-meaning.

Make sure you do all the usual checks for discomfort, like needing to be cuddled or fed or changed before you go any further. Remember, too, that you will be able to help your baby best if you can remain calm and endeavour to bring her down to a comfortable level of relaxation, rather than getting uptight yourself.

Cuddles, singing songs and 'walking the floor' are all tried and tested remedies – which incidentally provide just the right mixture of gentle *soothing* and *stimulation* to the senses.

In fact, any form of rhythmic movement and/or sound may help. A walk in the park could work wonders for both of you and you might bump into someone you know – a 'real human being' to talk to! Going out for a drive in the car may also be *soothing* for your baby, but please see also Avoiding Difference in Part 1 and, of course, **don't drive if you are feeling really uptight.**

If you cannot find any obvious reason for your infant's distress and if his crying is really getting to you, stay with him but try plugging into your personal stereo with your favourite tapes and let the headphones take some of the strain. That way you may both find relief and get through those difficult times together. Alternatively, choose a *soothing* tape you can both enjoy.

However, if it really feels too bad, make sure your baby is safe then get up and walk away. Make yourself a cup of tea, crack open a banana (for the energy, and for the potassium and serotonin, both of which can have a calming effect on your nervous system) and switch off for a few moments. Then, as soon as you feel ready, go back to your baby's side.

Since background 'white' noise can help to soothe some children, and doing the vacuuming or loading the washing machine could give you something constructive to do (and drown out the crying for just a few minutes), you could try getting on with some essential chores. If nothing else, you will feel better for having done something! Sing at the top of your voice as well, if it helps. **Please be aware of infants who are very sensitive to noise and, in any case, keep this up for VERY short periods only.** You will want to make regular checks on your baby every few minutes, or as soon as you have calmed down yourself.

It can be very comforting for your baby to be wrapped in a thick sheet, soft blanket or shawl, with her arms and legs left slightly bent and her hands free to move. This may help her to feel 'held' or **contained**, particularly at moments of anxiety or distress. You could continue to hold her in her little 'cocoon', or put her down once she is **soothed** enough to sleep. **Some very sensitive children, including some children who have been neglected or abused, may feel very threatened by being wrapped up in this way. Take care.**

One aspect many parents overlook is the necessity for our children to cry. Consider that each of our children has experienced at least one **traumatic** loss and has probably received some poor care in the womb, or after her birth. Only you can know, or guess at, the full history of your child's earliest days. What can be said for certain is that your little one needs to grieve her losses and let out her pain. Of course she is far too young to be consciously aware of these but she may sometimes show her distress by periodic crying, exaggerated body movements or even **withdrawal (dissociation)**.

Try to resist the natural urge to comfort your child by stopping her crying as soon as possible. On the contrary, give her permission to let go of the unconscious pain she is expressing whilst you hold her and keep her safe.

Very young humans are genetically programmed to cry, purely to ensure that their mothers (the **attachment figure**) stay close to them or return to care for them as soon as possible. It is a natural survival strategy which demands your close co-operation!

Tell your child that you know it was bad for her and that you are there for her now. At some deep level she will pick up, perhaps from your tone of voice or from your gentle, **containing** touch, that she is safe and that you feel for her. Letting out the painful feelings can help her to heal more quickly from the **trauma**, although it may feel more painful for us at the time. It is also from your sharing and **reflecting back** of feelings to your child that her foundations for learning **empathy** are laid down.

Forget the myth that a crying baby **necessarily** means an uncaring or careless parent. It is precisely because you do care that you are allowing her to cry through her inner pain. The difference now is that your baby is no longer alone and need no longer be terrified of being overwhelmed by her feelings.

Sleep Disturbances

Some little ones find it difficult to go to sleep, or to stay asleep. They may have difficulties **regulating** their **body rhythms** or levels of excitement/stress, or relaxing their vigilance against an expected **abandonment**, hurt or terror. By adopting a relaxed routine and employing strategies which **soothe** your child's senses, such as age-old rhythmic lullabies, soft lights, aromatherapy oils or gentle rocking, you may be able to help her feel calm enough and safe enough to 'let go'.

Familiar **transitional objects**, such as 'blankies', with their comforting feel and smell can be particularly useful in letting a young child move from wakefulness to sleep. (See also Avoiding Difference in Part 1.)

How your baby or toddler goes to sleep may affect whether he remains asleep or not. If he falls asleep in your arms, or crashes out on the sofa, he may well wake up as, or soon after, you put him into his own cot or bed. This may be because, in a lighter period of sleep, he is able to sense the change. It will probably be better if you put him to bed whilst he is still awake – but stay around (in the background) whilst he settles himself.

For some babies some level of background noise will be preferred, whilst some little ones cannot tolerate complete darkness. Using the Hoover or washing machine sometimes works, or you could try leaving a plug-light or a night-light (safely out of reach) in the corner of the room.

Many small children do not like being on their own, as this *kindles* their fears of *abandonment*. How do you feel about buying a bigger bed? **However, be sensitive about sharing beds where you believe your child may have been sexually abused, or may never have been given any space of his own.**

You could wrap up a small pillow in a familiar smelling old towel and tuck it in safely with your child (but away from her face) for extra reassurance. Wrapping your young child in a sheet or blanket can also be a useful adjunct to sleep (see also Section on Crying Babies on page 70).

Sometimes favourite lullabies, nursery rhymes or stories on tape (in your own voice, preferably) may help.

If you do need to go into your baby's room at night, **it is best not to switch bright lights on, unless you wish to switch your baby on as well!** Use a plug-light or night-light instead.

A few drops of essential oils such as lavender or chamomile in warm water or in a burner over a night light, safely out of reach of your baby, can help create a *soothing* effect. The pleasing aromas go straight to the part of the brain (within the *limbic system*) which *regulates* emotion and activity levels.

Some young children may be troubled by intrusive nightmares and *night terrors*, which they may not be able to recall or find words for. Again, your quiet presence, your gentle touch, your whispered, soothing words, your familiar smell, even a drink of water, may help to bring your child back from her state of terror.

With children for whom nightmares and *night terrors* are a problem, *sensory soothing,* such as cuddling, rocking, singing and stroking, can help them to reconnect with you and the reality of this safer world. The nightmares may be intrusive re-plays of specific earlier *traumatic* experiences, although their meaning may not at first be clear.

Since your young child's ability to recount the terrifying dream scenes, or to recall the original terror, may be poorly developed, you may need to help her find ways of expressing these, perhaps through sounds, drawing or play. This will be better approached in the morning, when she is fully awake and with you. If you know what happened to her early on, you may want to begin to talk to her about this at a more comfortable time. Be clear that you are on her side, that frightening things can happen but it is never her fault.

In the longer term, complementary therapies, such as cranial osteopathy, aromatherapy massage, homoeopathic and Bach flower remedies have been found to be very helpful with sleep disturbances. *Holding for nurture (holding time)* has been shown to help reduce *night terrors*, whilst *expressive therapies*, such as music, art, play and drama therapies, and *holding* and *attachment* therapies can help access the deeper memories, emotions and feelings which may underlie these sleep problems and which are beyond words (see also section on **'Safe holding'**).

Tantrums

A toddler wouldn't be a toddler without tantrums. Tantrums are part of the developmental process of moving from total dependence towards independence (which happens again in adolescence). Tantrums are all-pervading; little ones don't do 'em by half! This makes sense if we remember the infantile tendency to perceive events as intense sensations without beginning or end (see Part 4). Again, this polarised way of reacting to people and events can be seen in adolescents, who may throw their hearts completely into something or someone, only to hate them just as intensely within days! For the toddler, a tantrum is a way of attempting to deal with overwhelming feelings of helplessness and of being out of control. (See also Parts 5 and 6 on Grounding, Aggression and Siblings.)

Of course, the young child's tantrums can then appear to be all about who is in control, a battle of wills, rather than who feels out of control and needs some help to feel secure again. This pattern can be very exaggerated for some children, particularly if they have had *traumatic* experiences from which they have made assumptions about themselves as powerless and the world as chaotic or terrifying. Even a minor frustration or confusion may then lead to a head-on explosion against the world.

Behavioural psychologists tell us that behaviours which are given attention (*rewarded*) will persist, whilst those which are ignored (not rewarded) will soon fade out. Similarly, many child rearing 'experts' will recommend defusing or ignoring, whilst making safe, as the best methods of dealing with toddler tantrums. It certainly may be possible to distract some toddlers from the source of their frustrations – doing this in matter of fact, fun ways is definitely worth a try.

However, once a tantrum is in full stream, leaving your little one to handle his flood of feelings alone does not make theoretical or practical sense. There will be an automatic set of *physiological* responses, including *stimulation* of the heart, respiration and temperature rates (at the *brain stem* level) and increased arousal, in the *mid brain*, and *limbic system*. These will intensify the child's distress and make it more likely that such responses will happen again, since we have allowed him to re-experience those earliest overwhelming feelings of *abandonment*, helplessness, chaos and fear.

Instead you need to provide safety, comfort and connection in order to provide healthy, 'corrective emotional experiences' and to begin to re-programme his distorted patterns of *arousal*. **You may need to provide a *containing* experience of similar intensity if you are to reach him.**

Holding your child gently but firmly through a tantrum can be such a healing experience, since it communicates through the earliest sensory pathways and can directly access the areas of the brain which are associated with *self-regulatory* and *attachment* functions.

Don't rush into this with a child you know has problems with touch – you may have to go slowly at first. (See also Section on Encouraging Touch on page 49.)

A word about **anger**. We tend to think of anger in very negative terms, as something bad and dangerous. Certainly this is how our children may relate to anger. We often expend enormous amounts of energy holding in our anger, and yet it slips past us when we least expect it, when we are tired or under stress. We then feel guilty, which in turn makes us angry with ourselves or with others. However, anger can be a very positive, dynamic emotion. It can give us the strength and the motivation to challenge and to change. It is not anger *per se* which is bad; it is the harmful, destructive elements of anger which we all need to fight against. At the same time we can begin to foster the positive aspects of anger and harness them to the greater common good. It may be your justifiable anger at the suffering your little one has experienced which inflames you and empowers you to find ways of helping her to heal.

Eating Problems

Taking in food, as liquids or solids, is part of our earliest behaviour. Once separated from the umbilical cord, a baby very soon has to put lips to nipple or teat and suck(le) if she is to survive. It is because it is such a primitive and primary function that early *traumatic* disturbances can so profoundly and permanently alter patterns of eating. Once established, they may be some of the hardest behaviours to change. How many of us have tried over and over to diet, only to have an irresistable urge for fatty, sweet tasting foods when we are tired or stressed? We intrinsically *associate* feeling good with feeling nurtured and well nourished in babyhood: hence the attraction of milk substitutes and derivatives. Even non-nutritious ingestion or 'mouthing' of substances, such as smoking, may bear some relation to our original oral experiences.

Some children clearly have feeding difficulties from an early age. They may not have been fed consistently or in a nurturing way. Some little ones will then feed greedily, as if this might be their last meal, which may well have been almost the case in the past. As they get older they may also steal and hoard food. Others may have *never associated* feeding with human comfort or inner relief, for instance if they were fed with a bottle propped up in their cot, and may feed poorly and without obvious pleasure. Again, some children who have experienced rough handling, like having the bottle rammed into their mouths, or oral forms of sexual abuse, may be under- or over-sensitive to many things in their mouths. **It may take a long time for you to work out what is going on for them and to find ways of altering their responses.**

Keep meal times as low key as possible, to avoid inducing further anxieties. Set a regular routine of meal times and behaviours which every member of the family follows.

Try to provide small amounts of things your child seems to enjoy, and gradually introduce new tastes and textures, or less favoured foods, once you have begun to establish a healthier pattern of eating. **Again, stay aware of possible *triggers*, particularly if you believe your child could have been abused.** (See also Section on Encouraging Touch on page 49.)

Never force your youngster to eat up or finish anything, although you will want to get the message over that you will expect him to try. You may want to keep between-meal snacking to a minimum, to encourage better eating at appropriate times. This may mean that you worry he is not getting enough to eat at first, but do you really want to set up a pattern of picking and junk eating?

Find ways of making meal times fun for the child with a poor appetite. Relatively unlimited supplies of bread, milk, fruit and vegetables for children who never seem satisfied, may be effective in keeping them feeling full and letting them know that food will always be there, whilst simultaneously encouraging good eating choices.

Do watch out for particular cravings and dislikes, chewing or swallowing difficulties (see also Section on Encouraging Touch on page 49), **and physical or emotional and behavioural reactions to foods.** Even staples like milk and bread can cause allergic reactions and sensitivities in some children and kids often crave the very ones they need to avoid.

Be vigilant, too, for *kindling* reactions. The textures, smells, colours and so on, of certain foods may *trigger* memories of earlier *traumas* (custard, yogurt or lumpy food, for example may distress children who were maltreated, poorly nourished or orally abused). In this case avoid these *triggers* completely until you feel the little one is relaxed and can handle eating most things. You may then be able to begin to re-introduce the offensive items gradually, if you wish.

Talk to your child as much as you can about his body and the body feelings we have. You can touch his 'tummy' and say that it is where the food goes which fills us up. Explain that really being 'filled up' involves not just food and drink but also love, affection, caring and feeling good about ourselves.

You can begin to point out that he may need more help to find ways of feeling filled up, since he missed out so much when he was little. You could tell him he did the very best he could to get by when things were hard for him but that now he can begin to learn other ways of feeling satisfied and comforted with you.

Normalise his way of coping by talking about how we all comfort eat/fail to feed ourselves well when we are very upset and show him ways you cope with that yourself.

Regression

Your youngster may spontaneously slip back into younger patterns of behaviour when she first comes home, or when she feels distressed. Don't worry, be patient, this won't last for ever. In addition, even very young children may need to go back and 'fill in the gaps' in their early lives. There may be times when you will wish actively to encourage this, for her greater emotional well-being. Of course, she may *regress* just at the time when you least want or expect this, when your social worker visits or the grandparents arrive! **Try not to get upset, or you may *trigger* further distressed or distressing behaviours.**

Knowing that *regression* is an important developmental strategy, you could take the initiative and set aside regular times when 'being a baby' is fine. The rest of the time you will be expecting behaviour which is as age-appropriate as she can manage. **Remember that you may still not always get this, and don't let it become a battle!**

Having the opportunity to play with younger children is a perfect opportunity for planned *regression*. A child may also interact better with non-family members, since they may be seen as less threatening to her tenuous sense of belonging and security. **For impulsive or aggressive youngsters you will need to be watchful and make sure that smaller children are not put at risk** but if you can manage it, it can be very healing.

Do you remember Harlow's monkeys? The ones reared apart from their mothers were anti-social and aggressive. One of the Harlows' co-workers (Alan Sroufe) set about trying to rehabilitate these youngsters. He found that the only effective method was to put them with 'normal' immature monkeys, so that they learned sociability naturally. He found that they still tended to act more aggressively under intense stress but in reasonable situations they had learned to behave reasonably.

Contact with small, and larger, furry animals can have a similar effect. Not only does the child have the chance to have fun, but research has clearly shown the calming effects of stroking pets on the heart and respiratory rates. That's *modulation* of *arousal* at the level of the *brain stem*! **Please remember that you need to be sure of the animals' safety at all times.**

Aggression

This is a very difficult area for many people, both to understand and to live with. Some physical expressions of frustration and anger are to be expected from little ones: they are, after all, only children. But living with an aggressive child is something different, something which many people have not experienced, cannot believe, or may only see as a vulnerable child's response to living in a dysfunctional family. (See also sections on Grounding (page 69), Tantrums (page 74), and Siblings (page 91).)

In the case of adopted and foster children, other people may be seeing only part of the life picture, picking up on the current family system and overlooking the *traumatic* effects of their pasts. Others will acknowledge the problem but take a 'wait and see' approach, assuming it is 'just a phase she will grow out of'. Whilst it is vital that you do not over-react to any indications of aggression and start labelling your youngster as an irredeemable psychopath, it is worth remembering that the best known predictor of adult violent behaviours is aggressive or destructive behaviours in early childhood.

Nobody likes a biter, a kicker or a bully. Other children, even little ones, will want to have nothing to do with a child who shouts, hurts, torments, threatens or frightens them. Aggressive children soon become known to teachers and parents alike. They can easily become excluded from invitations, outings and activities and even blamed for things they didn't do, because of their reputations. This generates a vicious circle, in which a child who has not learned to contain his natural feelings of anger and is struggling to find a comfortable *sense of self*, will receive predominantly negative feedback from his interactions and will continue to feel alienated, *hurt* and angry.

As parents of aggressive youngsters, you may also be faced with your own feelings of frustration, anger, *hurt*, even revenge, against this child who disturbs your equilibrium so fiercely. You may also feel embarrassed that a child of yours could act this way, feel responsible for the upsets she causes, and ostracised and blamed by parents of other children who have been *hurt* or frightened. **It is at this point that it is vital to remember the overwhelming *physiological*, *bio-chemical* and *psychological* effects of early trauma.** Your child has been so *hurt*, *psychically* or *physically*, in her past that she struggles to feel good about herself, has relationship and *attachment* difficulties, finds *self-regulation* difficult, and her responses are easily *triggered* by relatively minor incidents. **It is emphatically not your fault, but neither should you blame the child for being 'bad'. You do, however, need to accept responsibility for helping her to learn new ways of functioning and dealing with her very powerful, destructive feelings.**

Once again, the way forward can be found in handling strategies which address the *regulatory areas* of the brain directly. Your *hurt* child will also need extremely good role models who can sustain a calm, reflective approach under duress! This can be very hard, when faced with seeming mayhem, but it is essential if your little one is to heal. **A *hurt* and *hurting* youngster is a victim as much as she may be a victimiser and needs all the security, *containment*, closeness and understanding you can give her right now.** Commentators on child behaviour who see aggression as a socially learned behaviour are partly right: learning does take practice alongside others. So the more your child can practise feeling comfortable with herself, and the less time she spends practising *hurting* other people, the better.

Remember that most of this rage is not meant for you, even though it may seem that way. For your own well-being you need to take this on board, if you are going to survive yourself and help your child to heal.

Forget what you may have heard about ignoring unwanted behaviours – the child doesn't want to feel like this either but he knows no other way of communicating or reacting. He needs your help to find out right now.

Try to nip aggressive patterns in the bud. Small children, and bigger ones, tend to begin with a low level of annoying behaviour and gradually build up to a major outburst if left unchallenged. Defusing a potential time bomb, perhaps with a controlled explosion, is better than hoping it won't go off!

You could try bringing humour into the situation, since laughter can alter stress levels and has been shown to be therapeutic in many clinical, as well as family, situations.

Alternatively, a little friendly rough and tumble may be all you need to interrupt the pattern. You are, quite literally, getting in touch and encouraging acceptable forms of physical self-expression.

Always work to bring your child's level of *arousal* down to a reasonable level using your own as a guide.

Keep your voice and your body language as unthreatening as possible. For example, sitting down with your knees apart, arms open and welcoming, and speaking in a soft, clear voice can let your child know directly that you are not going to *hurt* him. **Take control, don't lose it.**

Use *holding for nurture* (see Section on Safe Holding on page 69) both on a regular basis and, if necessary, when things get too hot. Be the *container* and the sounding board for your child's confused feelings. Help him to recognise what is going on inside, without in any way denying or minimising his pain.

Let him know that his angry feelings are understandable, that you would feel angry if you had been *hurt*, rejected, abused, neglected by the people who were supposed to love you.

At the same time, give the message that hurting other people is not acceptable, nor will it make him feel better about himself in the long run. You may want to use more direct, physical ways of releasing the anger, such as beating up pillows, kneading bread dough, stamping through puddles, kicking up leaves, banging pots and pans together, screaming down drainpipes, running in the wind. This helps the body as well as the mind to learn new ways to respond safely, without cutting off or denying the feelings. By sharing the intensity of feelings, you are likely to increase your connection with your child.

Similarly, after the crisis you will probably both feel tired and relieved. If you can, spend some quiet time together now, to capitalise on the 'resolution' phase of the *rage cycle* and to consolidate your connections.

When he is calm, talk to your child about what went on, helping him to make *associations* between what went on just before the blow-up and what he felt and did – in the outside world and inside his body and head. A rage reaction is frequently a *dissociative* reaction.

Watch out for what it is which sets your child's anger off. The underlying elements are likely to be fear, heightened anxiety and a feeling of helplessness. It may well look to you like sheer mean-ness or cussedness on your child's part but, to begin with at least, it is a *trauma* response pure and simple.

Notwithstanding that, you do not have to tolerate aggressive behaviour to show him that you love him. **Accepting unacceptable behaviour does your child, yourself and your family no favours.** Showing him that you will *not* let him hurt you, or himself, is far more loving and empowering for all of you than allowing him further practice in *hurting*. **The sooner the pattern of violent responses is changed the better.**

Remember to allow yourself space to recover from each explosive outburst, or you too will run the risk of staying 'hyped up' and vulnerable to *post-traumatic stress reactions*. A few minutes spent away from your youngster are sometimes essential and will show him that you can remain safely in control. Whether you go for complete peace and quiet (?), or a brief burst of energetic movement, make it fun. (See also Section on Grounding on page 66.)

Always try to make sure other children (and pets) stay safe. Help them to find a secure place to go to, perhaps up to their own bedroom or to see the next door neighbour, if you think the aggressive outburst is likely to take some time to work through. You may need to give your other children permission to defend themselves and their possessions (as non-violently as possible), even if they are older and bigger than your aggressive little one. By helping them to stand up for themselves you are teaching them not to be victims and teaching your young child the way it is in the real world. (See also Section on Siblings on page 91.)

Encouraging Children to Know and Show Their Feelings

Some children who have experienced early separations, losses, and *hurts* have never come to recognise their own feelings, or may not have had the opportunity to express those feelings safely. On the surface they may seem very 'together' or *self-possessed*. In fact their predominant pattern may be one of *dissociating*, of *switching off* from the world, or from parts of themselves which feel dangerous. Far from being *self-possessed* they are *self-dispossessed* and *hurting* very deeply inside their protective shells.

Your youngster may feel, at some very deep level, that she does not exist at all beneath this facade of competence. She may be over-sensitive to the slightest irritation or rejection from you, interpreting this as further proof that nobody cares about her and that she is bad. That is the way it was for her when she was very small. What other conclusion can a small child draw than that she *hurts* because she is not good enough to be loved? She could not bear the thought that the adults on whom she depended were not perfect: that would threaten her entire existence.

As parents of such young children it can be difficult to handle your own confused emotions in response to the child, to break through the veneer, and to reach the real *child within*. Your child may fight you tooth and nail to retain the defensive patterns which kept her 'safe' against the emptiness, the *hurts*, the insults of her early life. **It will take more than time and love to alter these patterns of a lifetime.** However, remember once again that you can always handle what you can understand: the challenge then shifts to how?!

Here, perhaps more than for any other difficulties, you may have to rely solely on your inner judgement that things are not quite right. A child who smiles sweetly and does what she is told, is undemanding, or goes off and spends time on her own is every parent's dream, surely? (See also Section on The "Charming Offensive" on page 85.) However, your gut feeling may tell you this doesn't feel right. If your child has not worked through the earlier developmental stages of total dependency, mutual interaction and the need for others, and has clearly not begun to be in touch with her own body and feelings, then it is very likely that your child *does* have a significant problem.

Your main aim here will always be to provide additional stimulation, and new and healing experiences, against a background of security, consistency and love, to try to make good the effects of early *hurts*. Sometimes this may seem like a contradiction in terms: but at times we need to be contradictory to produce change. The secret is in balancing the child's need to experience the familiar and predictable against the equally vital need to challenge what has become familiar and expected: the expectation that she will be ignored, rejected, *abandoned* and *hurt*, if she allows herself to become vulnerable, or to get close. **Too little, and she may stay where she is, locked in her own world; too much, and she may be overwhelmed and withdraw further.**

So keep in mind that every child needs safety, warmth, touch, closeness, movement and comfort and begin gently to find, and push back, her limits of tolerance in every way you can.

Gradually raise your child's levels of activity, intimacy and interest, remembering to build in (comparable) levels of calm and relaxation to follow. *Stimulation* and *soothing* are the twin corner-stones by which the *good enough* mother helps her infant move toward greater *associations* at the deepest levels.

The more novel and surprising you can make the activities, without *over-stimulation*, the better, since they will selectively grab her attention, in preference to familiar objects and situations.

Keep reminding yourself and your child that he is not to blame for how he is. Give him messages that you expect him to change gradually, that you are with him all the way and that you intend to have fun in the process.

Continue to use *holding time* as much as you can. (See section on Safe Holding on page 69.) This allows you to work at the earliest developmental levels and potentially alter your child's earliest beliefs about himself and the world.

Encourage your child to make noises and movements that symbolise how he does feel, without criticism, fear, disgust or trying to change anything. Acceptance and *empathy* are much more valuable messages, which he will need to keep on hearing over and over again.

As your youngster grows, give him chances to make shapes or models, with play dough for example, or to scribble or paint what it is like inside his body and his head. He may communicate much through the intensity of motion, texture or colour, or even his mutterings and body positions as he works. Words come later.

Model your own feelings and emotions in very exaggerated ways. Find toys with sad, happy, confused faces (do they make them with angry faces?). **Tell your child how you think they may be feeling or demonstrate ways of managing those feelings for the toys.**

Introduce the same sort of concepts in relation to the child himself. No-one may ever have acknowledged or accepted his feelings, or named them or talked about them. In fact his survival was probably based on the converse: secrecy, denial and staying silent. **Show him that you can hear and hold all he has to say.**

Find little books in which very young children are featured and where their feelings are given prominence. The Althea books are simple and well written. The Mr. Men series (including the Little Misses and ignoring the patent sex stereotyping) are also great for making all sorts of feelings acceptable: Mr. Grumpy for uncomfortable feelings, Mr. Bump for 'clumsiness' and so on. (See also reviews of booklets for very young children who have been abused in back copies of *Adoption UK*, the bi-monthly magazine of Adoption UK.)

You could introduce the concepts of warmth and cold, which we often use metaphorically, to refer to relationships and the feelings we get from them. Ask your child to put his hand on a warm radiator, sit in a sunny spot, eat a warm bread bun, or wrap him in a cosy shawl. Then, for contrast, get him to hold a cube of ice, or to put his toes in cold water.

You can take the symbol of an ice cube further. Since your little one is attempting to stay safe by avoiding warmth and intimacy, and he may also be deeply afraid that there is nothing inside, he can see for himself that the ice is not lost when it melts, merely transformed into liquid. You may be able to show him that water is much more friendly, flexible and fun than ice. Eventually you could even demonstrate that getting upset and 'all steamed up' is not the end of the world either, since you can catch the steam and allow it to condense back into water droplets. Nothing is really lost in the changes that he sees, and it is the same for all of us. We can choose to be any of these things, to try something else, and to change back again if we wish.

The 'Charming Offensive'

There are some young children who seem to smile all the time. They smile at anyone, anywhere, and when they smile at you, they seem to smile through you. Often a child like this has had to learn to smile at all costs in order to survive. In large orphanages with small numbers of staff, it may be the smiling baby who gets picked up, fed or talked to. Within an abusive or neglectful family a little one may wear a smile to hide the fear, to placate an angry parent or to please her molester. **Since** smiling is a socially accepted and acceptable behaviour universally, it can be very difficult to alter this pattern when the 'winning smile' no longer suits the game.

It is probably the total lack of understanding from other people, casual acquaintances, or old ladies in supermarkets, which makes dealing with this one particularly stressful. The smile charms everyone so much that it continues to bring its own rewards to your child, and almost everyone else but you. **Trust your own instincts!** If it doesn't feel right to you, then it very probably is not right for your child. As the closest person to your child, you are the one who is most tuned into her and is most likely to sense the real discomfort hiding behind the mask of a smile. **Keep reminding yourself of this when it starts getting to you.**

Try to resist the urge to beat all the 'smitten' adults over the head with your umbrella! They don't know what is really going on for your child as you do. It could help to have a quick image in your head of 'zapping' them and then bring yourself back to reality. Remind yourself that at least your child has made someone's day today. Perhaps tomorrow it will be yours!

It is also essential that you avoid putting your child down in front of these 'outsiders', or showing irritation to the 'innocents' who have been 'conned'. Not only is this *hurtful* to your child, it can only make you look more like 'the Wicked Witch of the West'!

Again, it may help you to keep in mind that, however frustrating it feels to you, this is a pattern of behaviour which helped your *hurt* child to cope and to get this far. **Although letting it go will be difficult, she will be able to do it – with your help and when she feels safe enough to try things a different way.**

You may wish to seek specialist help from a therapist familiar with traumatised and neglected children to help you unlock your child's inner feelings, as well as working with her at home. A drama, music, play or art therapist may be able to help your child to connect with her buried feelings, where a 'talk' therapist may not.

As much as possible, **try to exaggerate your own facial expressions relating to your feelings and tell your child quite clearly how you feel.** The more over the top you can be on this one the better! Get all your family and friends on your side and ask each of them to join you in this. The more your little one can be exposed to *modelling* of real feelings, the more she will make the connections and know that her own feelings are acceptable.

Of course it is highly likely that she has no idea of how she feels inside, since she has not had adequate opportunities to learn. Not only will you have to 'give her permission' to feel, by your own example, but you will also have to begin to tease out and name her feelings for her. (See also Section on Encouraging Feelings on page 82.)

You could play at making faces. Focus on sad faces, puzzled faces, angry faces and laughing faces. 'Simon's Face Says' could be an appropriate alternative to the standard version of the game.

Draw 'sad, mad, glad and scared' faces on balloons and allow them to float around and 'talk'. Then ask your child to take hold of one and give it a voice, or a sound or a movement.

When you see the set smiling face, tell your child what you see on the outside and what you believe you can see on the inside. Remind her that if it is only the mouth that smiles and not the eyes, then it is not a 'real' smile. Use a mirror to try and get across the difference.

You could make a big fuss of touching your child, examining her all over and listening to her chest. Whisper that you can hear a very small, quiet voice inside, asking to be let out. Encourage your child to talk to this *inside child part*. You can tell your youngster that you know how very *hurt* she is inside and how dangerous it must feel to her. Help her to begin to feel it is safe to let her *inside child parts* out too.

If your child cannot find a voice for her *inside child*, perhaps you could give her one to begin with.

You could try using a teddy or doll to represent your child. Give the doll your child's name and show your child how you are able to take great care of such a special, frightened child. You could try telling her that you intend to go on looking after the doll in this way until she is able to look after it herself.

Make a great game out of nurturing the doll and pretending to listen to her crying. Your child will see you *modelling empathy* for her baby *self* and may be able to get in touch with her inner feelings more directly.

Get hold of some hand puppets. Your child may feel safer playing and talking through a 'third person' than when you focus on her directly. **Sometimes addressing a child directly can** *trigger* **a fear or** *shame* **reaction, which may in turn lead to a** *dissociative* **response, particularly in a child who is so out of touch with herself already.**

There are some specialist toys available which might help your child relate to the *hurt child within*, for example a rabbit which shivers, a doll with a small crying baby doll inside. These tangible symbols may put her in touch more directly with her true *self.*

Last of all, take your time, and don't expect miracles overnight!

Encouraging Children Who Seem Too Afraid to Ask for What They Need

In the normal development of infants and toddlers, the anxiety of separation leads a child to return to the safety of the mother figure, either physically, visually through eye contact, or verbally. Every child has to go through this *separation anxiety* stage and practise lengthening separations as she matures, in order to move on to healthy independence. If the separations come too soon, are too prolonged, or are too overwhelming, then the child may respond by becoming increasingly clingy (*anxious, insecure attachment*), withdrawn (*avoidant*), may swing between these two patterns of interaction (*ambivalent*) or, *very* infrequently, become totally unconnected to others (*unattached*). Since the child feels powerless in the world, she does this to try to gain an (illusory) sense of control over her life and her surroundings.

Lack of consistent comfort from previous *primary caregivers* (birth parents, foster parents, hospital, residential or orphanage carers) has not allowed such children to feel secure in others and themselves, or to establish predictable life patterns. They may never have developed any real sense of their own bodily needs and certainly will have little trust that anyone else but themselves will give them what they want. **The little ones who show the** *withdrawn, avoiding, 'switched off'* **or** *compliant* **pattern may need a lot of extra help before they are able to let you know what they really need.**

Start by going back to basics, to establish *basic trust*, permanence and *awareness of self.* Beyond this, anything you can do to encourage your youngster to practise being dependent on you, and activities which enable her to refer back to you often, can pay dividends in the long run.

Use meal times, snack times and play times to establish the routine of asking and replying, giving and receiving. Get everyone in your family to ask for everything! **Take care to avoid any hint of irritability or anxiety around the meal table, especially if eating is already experienced as stressful by your child.** Keep it light and keep it fun! (See also Section on Eating Problems on page 75.)

You could begin by playing at being a baby. You be the baby, cry, wriggle, pull sad or angry faces. Ask her what she thinks you might need. If she is able to tell you, ask her how she knows. If not, do the talking for her. Reverse the roles and play it again.

Alternatively, you could use teddy or dolly or a hand puppet to be the 'asker', which can make the asking one step removed from your child himself and therefore easier to begin with.

Story time can always be a good opportunity for 'requests'. You are likely, naturally, to ask 'which one do you want to hear today?' Make it easier by offering only two or three clear choices. Similarly, simple choices about which clothes to put on, or which cereal to eat, can also lead your child into feeling he has some choices in, and therefore some control over, his life. You may want to give him the asking words yourself first and then gradually encourage him to add his own.

Playing at 'shop' can cultivate the ability to ask for what he needs. Take turns and *model* good ways to ask yourself.

'Mother May I' games are also good fun. You could introduce a humorous element by joining in with ridiculous requests and responses. Not only can this make the game more enjoyable, it can also get your child thinking!

School playground games such as 'What's the Time Mr. Wolf?' and 'Sly Fox' can encourage your growing child to turn round for reference, where looking and asking patterns remain weak.

Be a robot and insist on asking for instructions before every movement. The more wooden and jerky you are the better.

Make an old fashioned string and cocoa tin telephone. Get your child to radio in and ask you for things that way. There may be less stress involved when there's a little distance between you. (See also 'piggy backs' and 'horsey rides' in section on 'Encouraging awareness of movement'.)

Special Difficulties Within Your Family

On Being Parents

Sometimes your child seems to show more distress with the *primary caregiving* parent than with the other parent. Often it is the close relationship with the *mothering figure* which seems surrounded by anxiety, whilst the infant may seem quite comfortable about being handled by the other parent, usually the father. This can begin a spiral of tension between the child and the less favoured parent *and* between the partners. The feeling is that one is 'getting it right' and the other is not. There is then a natural enough temptation to hand over care as much as possible to the one whom the child seems to have accepted.

While this may be a helpful short-term strategy, so that both mother and child can experience the least possible stress as they begin to relate, it is not a good long-term solution. The mother–child *attachment* relationship is the first and most important relationship for your child. Failure to establish this primary relationship could mean that your child will continue to have difficulty with close relationships throughout his life. It may be because your small child has somehow learned to be afraid of getting close that he feels more comfortable with someone other than his mother, the person who is trying to do just that: get close.

Initially the father's principal role is to be there for the mother and to support her in an intimate bond with the child. As time goes by you will have the opportunity to form a sound *attachment* relationship with the infant yourself and to lead him towards the 'big, wide world' beyond Mum. The world is then your, and your child's, oyster!

In the meantime you could try having 'family cuddles', in which Mum holds baby and Dad holds Mum. Dad can talk to the baby, and touch him and stroke him but Mum is doing the holding. Even when the child is openly rejecting you as the mother, keep in mind that it is in his best interests to experience closeness with you first.

Being pushed away, being ignored or bringing on rageful crying when you pick up or handle your baby does not feel good. It can test your belief in yourself to the limit. **Try always to keep in mind that it is not you who is 'doing it wrong' when your child reacts badly to your *soothing* and caring.**

Perhaps you could ask yourself 'Do I want my child to grow up unable to be cuddled or to get close?' The only way your little one will be able to find out that being held is the best thing in the world, is to experience it himself. Hold on if things don't seem too good at first, they can only get better!

Children who have been neglected or physically or sexually abused may have particular problems with touch and closeness. **You must respect this wariness (it has kept them alive this far) but you must also respect their right for a complete life. Life without close *attachments* is far from complete.**

Siblings

Jealousy between children in a family is extremely common, even if it is unpleasant to live with. However, children who have been *hurt* in the past, who have experienced separations, losses, neglect or abuse, often find it much harder to share anything – particularly their parents and their personal space.

If you have taken a sibling group into your family there may already be difficulties which have resulted from favouring or 'scapegoating' one or more of the children in their family of origin. Take time to talk in depth to previous carers, to try to find out what seems to be going on between the children. In some cases one child may be physically or sexually abusing another sibling. In this case he is probably identifying with the adult who has *hurt* him and trying to take control of his own chaotic life in the only way he knows. **Whilst this is completely understandable, it cannot be allowed to continue, for the other child(ren)'s sake as well as his own.**

Even children who have come home to your family individually, when they were very young, may show some of these difficulties. **If it is at all possible, try to leave several years between additions to the family, whether they come through adoption or are 'home grown' children.**

Just because **we** love all our children, it doesn't mean that all our children are naturally going to love each other. **Telling your youngster that you love him so much you are going to have another child may make perfect sense to you but not to him.** Try thinking of this in a different way. How would you feel if your child told you he was going to get another Mum and Dad because he loved you so much!?

You may feel torn apart by the struggles and fights which go on between your children. You may begin to feel guilty that it is your fault – that if only you hadn't wanted another child this wouldn't have happened. In families built by adoption you may be particularly likely to feel this way.

Whatever the circumstances, guilt will get you nowhere! Taking responsibility for solving a problem you could not have foreseen is much more worthwhile.

Do your best to give enough time to each child, whilst remembering that 'enough' is like a piece of string – how long is it?

It is probably better not to insist that your children share their things. If you can, give each a defined space which is 'their own'. This could be a bedroom, or a corner of the living room, or a box in the playroom. **Where a child has experienced sexual abuse, the bedroom may not feel a safe or private place to be.**

Named hooks for coats and regular places at the meal table are also a good idea. If necessary label *everything*, in the short term! You can always use pictures for pre-school children, or even colour coding.

If you can, make time to do favourite things with each child individually. You will probably find that even the most challenging child will be 'sweetness and light' for a short while, given your undivided attention and something fun to do. You both deserve that!

Don't, on the other hand, exhaust yourself and forgo time for yourself which you need to meet the inevitably insatiable demands of two or more small children. You will all benefit from short periods apart, as long as you handle them sensitively.

Nor should you try to do exactly the same things with each child. For one thing it is impossible and, for another, each child's needs are different. Remember that whatever you do, each child will always feel 'it isn't fair' at some point. Life isn't always fair and some (minor) frustrations are probably necessary in this life.

If there are nasty feelings between your children, you will need to make sure that the smallest, or the most vulnerable, can trust you to take care of them. **Even very small children may try to protect you from their feelings, or feel that they should 'put up and shut up', especially if they have already been *hurt* themselves.**

Youngsters will also benefit greatly from being shown ways of taking care of themselves. You are setting them a good example (***modelling***) every time you take care of yourself. In addition you may need actively to encourage 'tale-telling' or offer them some way of letting you know when they feel threatened by their brother or sister.

You could give them a whistle, which they can blow when things get heavy, or get them to practise screaming or running away. You may feel that this is encouraging them to 'make a fuss' – yes it is! **Being bullied or threatened or teased or tormented is very likely to cause your small child to feel helpless and afraid to move or make a noise.** That is a *trauma* reaction which you will want to avoid.

Bigger children may try to be reasonable and tend to give in to a smaller trouble-maker, which is not good for either of them in the long run. Again you will want to let the non-offending child know that you can understand their frustrations and don't expect them to be saints. A small lock on the older child's bedroom door, or a designated 'older child only' space, can be very useful.

Dealing with the offending child (whether bigger or smaller than his victim) is also problematic. **At all costs do not get into punishment, especially physical or *hurtful* verbal punishments.** Not only will this leave you feeling bad, it could make the victimised child feel guilty and it will certainly legitimise the victimiser's use of violence in his own mind. (See also sections on Tantrums and Aggression on pages 74 and 78 respectively.)

Time out, or 'thinking time' (any time your child spends on his own at your request) can be useful at this point. This allows the *hurting, hurtful* child to begin to calm down and get in touch with his own feelings and the rest of you to 'lick your wounds'. **Keep these periods short and do not use them as punishment.**

Talking about why teasing or tormenting or *hurting* is not acceptable and reminding a child of his own inner *hurts* may need to be repeated over and over – and **only done when the child has calmed down.**

Sometimes even little children may deny what they have been doing – despite the evidence! **It may be that this is part of a *dissociative* pattern, that is the child may deny to himself that he did it and cannot really remember doing it.** He may be dealing with the confusion inside by making these behaviours 'not me', that is *dissociating* the 'bad' behaviours from his awareness.

Here you will have to be your child's external witness and conscience and tell him quietly and calmly what he has just done. **This, too, needs to wait until your child (and you) are feeling reasonable and calm.** You stand much more chance of accessing his thinking brain if he is not 'hyped up' or 'spaced out'.

You may feel that your child does these things deliberately. There may, indeed, be an element of intention about his actions but at the same time part of him may not want to be doing these things nor wish to acknowledge his *hurtful* side. **However out of control your child feels inside, he has to know that you can take safe control for him and that he can begin to take responsibility himself for ALL his actions.**

Holding your child at this time can help to give him these messages at non-verbal, as well as verbal, levels. He may feel that he is 'evil', not like everyone else. By *holding* him you tell him he is *not* untouchable and that you can help him to feel safe. Bringing down his obviously high level of anxiety means that he can begin to feel and function reasonably. This will then allow him to start putting the essential thinking space in before he acts next time. (See also Section on Safe Holding on page 69.)

Always try to find some way of communicating to your child that you know he has a 'good' side as well as a part which *hurts* other people.

You could invent 'smart buttons', perhaps on his forehead above each eye. Tell your youngster that by pressing there gently, you (and eventually he) can take control of his nasty feelings *and* get in touch with his 'good' *part*, the *part* who doesn't want to be *hurtful*.

Take care not to deny the reality of the 'bad' *part* or to imply it is somehow separate. For children who have learned to *dissociate*, this may entrench their perception of *parts* of themselves as 'not me'.

Talking about your child's own past *hurts*, at quiet times, can be very healing. You don't always need to be very specific (especially if you lack the information) but try not to minimise how much he has been *hurt* by other people. Inside, part of your child already knows this. Your validation will help him make sense of the turmoil and pain within – which he so often throws outside, when he tries to be *hurtful* to other children.

In part, it is the other child's vulnerability which may trigger your child's outbursts, since it reminds him, at some level, of his own earlier powerlessness and pain. *Hurting* someone else may be the only way he has known to feel in control or to release an unbearable build up of emotional tension. **It is important to remember that EXPLAINABLE behaviour is not necessarily EXCUSABLE behaviour – and this kind of aggression is never excusable.**

If you feel that this is a big problem for your family, do not be afraid to ask for outside help. A good psychotherapist or psychologist could help your young child work more directly through his own *hurts* and work with you to make home a secure and comfortable place to be for everyone.

Contact with Birth Families and Other Significant Figures from the Past

This is always an individual issue which needs very careful consideration for each child. However poorly the birth family has cared for your small child, they were, and always will be, part of her. You should never be afraid to speak about them or to try and find some tangible reminders of those earliest years. There are, however, many factors which may influence how, how much and what form of contact with significant people from your child's past is comfortable for you and your child.

People's understanding of what contact means may vary greatly. It can be anything from an annual card via a third party 'letterbox', all the way through to regular face-to-face meetings with the birth family, including extended family members. It may bring up many issues for all parties involved and it is often quite difficult to foresee just when and how these will occur. **It is therefore** essential that you establish, from the outset, that everyone's motives are as clear as possible and that they focus primarily on the needs and best interests of your child. Having an experienced third party to mediate contact is often advisable. Of course, circumstances can change, so a flexible approach is a *must*, just as long as the prime objective is your child's well-being.

For children who were abandoned, or placed in orphanages without formal documentation, it may be impossible for you to maintain even the most tenuous contact with families of origin. In this case, maintaining some continuity through contact with other significant figures from the past, including the police or nursing staff initially involved in handling your child, or residential caregivers and administrative personnel, may be the best you can do at present. Keeping the lines open from the beginning is always going to be easier than trying to track people down after several years: you need to assume that your child may one day wish to find out more about herself.

Don't be afraid to acknowledge the gaps in your child's life, with appropriate feelings of sadness or frustration, but remember it isn't your fault that things happened this way. In most cases there will have been some very pressing social or economic reasons why birth parents have apparently 'vanished into the blue'. If you suspect that some degree of institutionalised corruption took place, or systematic pressure was placed on parents unaware of their rights or unable to afford to keep their baby, this too is information which your child will need to know in time, at a level she can understand. However, feeling guilty about this, or dubious about your rights to bring up your child, can only get in the way of your relationship with her: you will need to find ways of letting go of those doubts, since there is almost nothing you can do about it at this stage. Perhaps, at a later date, you and your child can do something positive to try to influence the social and political structures of her home-land.

Whether or not you feel there were valid reasons for her being placed for adoption, bear in mind that your child may feel justifiably *hurt* and angry, at a very deep level. The only (unconscious) conclusion that a child may draw from such an *abandonment* is that she is bad, and does not deserve good care. To be treated so insensitively, or to live without acknowledgement, may leave a baby feeling that she does not have a right to exist, or does not really belong anywhere. This can also be the case when the pregnancy was unwanted or concealed. **You may have to work very hard, over an extended period, to counter these beliefs, which are fundamental to so many adopted children.**

Where neglect, abuse or gross inconsistency of care is an issue, it may be difficult for you to feel comfortable with encouraging any contact for your child with his birth family. You may feel so angry with the family who caused your child such pain, even if it was unintentional, that you feel you cannot tolerate the idea of their remaining in your child's life – perhaps likely to cause *hurt* all over again. If this is the case, say so. It is up to the agencies involved, and the birth family members themselves, to provide adequate justification for keeping in touch, otherwise your child may pick up on your ambivalence, even if he seems O.K. about contact himself.

Remember, however, that NOT ALL family members may have known of, or contributed to, your child's maltreatment. Often other extended family members, and grandparents in particular, may have a lot to offer your child, including on-going information and validation of her life.

Keeping in touch with siblings can also be very helpful, although there may be specific difficulties if some siblings have remained with the birth family, or have been placed in families in very different circumstances. Some foster and adoptive parents may not feel able to agree to brothers and sisters keeping in touch, or may have very different views on what is acceptable – in terms of information shared or the management of contact.

A child who has been sexually abused may also have particular concerns about their birth family. **Since sexual abuse always involves secrecy and denial, and frequently involves implicit or explicit threats (including the loss of love),** you need to respect your child's feelings and trust your own judgement about just how much information or contact is offered.

Since a young child cannot tolerate the idea that her parents, the only meaningful people in her life, could be *hurtful* or bad, she has to take all the *hurt* and badness into herself. She can then go on loving, and depending on, her abusive, neglectful or rejecting parents, whilst *dissociating* the awareness of the suffering. Your youngster may therefore hold on to an idealised image of her family, and continually struggle to get back to them, even though she knows at some level they have *hurt* her. She may even experience your caring as threatening, since her thinking is so distorted by the life she has already known.

This 'ambivalent attachment to the perpetrator' can be very confusing to everyone and you will have to work hard to help your child untangle her muddles. **Do not be pushed into believing that your child should really be back with her** *hurtful* **family or that she doesn't really need you.**

In this kind of abusive situation, any form of contact, be it photographs, cards, letters, phone calls or visits, may be just too confusing for a young child to handle. **Moreover, re-offending behaviours by abusers, including the perpetuation of 'our special relationship', or of veiled threats, is very common. This could allow your child to go on being** *traumatised* **and actively undermine your own developing relationships.**

On the other hand, contact with non-offending family members **who accept the reality of what has happened** can be helpful and supportive. This gives your child messages that other people in her family still want to know her, that they do not blame her for what has happened, and that it is not because she was bad that she can no longer live with them. Siblings, in particular, may be able to validate what happened to your child and, if they were abused as well, can help her feel she was not, and is not, alone. **Caution is required if you know, or suspect, that older siblings were actively involved in the abuse of the younger children.**

Whatever you decide to do about contact, please take as much time as you need to think things through thoroughly. Do not be swayed by pressures from well-intentioned professionals who believe that contact is always, or never, the right thing for a child. It is, after all, *you* who have to go on living with your child after an upsetting birthday card, an expensive present or an exciting trip out. (For further reading on this issue see the Adoption UK leaflet entitled *Maintaining Links with Birth Families*.)

Encouraging Life-Story Work

It is perhaps even more important for young children who have not had an easy, straight-forward start in life to know as much as they can about themselves as early as possible. They cannot begin to make sense of what has happened to them, an essential element of healing from *trauma*, if they don't know their own stories. **What a child does not know she may well invent, and the fantasies are often far worse than the reality.**

There are several excellent texts on life story books, such as *Life Story Work* by Tony Ryan and Rodger Walker, and Regina Kupecky's booklet for Romanian children, to which you can refer. (See the Reading List at the end of the book.)

Sadly, we as parents often have very little real information to work with. Details may not have been seen as important enough to record, or may subsequently have been overlooked in report writing. Suspicions of maltreatment are often left out if they have not been substantiated, or minimised so as not to cause distress (to whom?). You, yourselves, may have been so excited to know you were going to have a child, that, understandably, you were unable to pay attention to all the information you were being given. Or you thought it would all come right once the child was with you. Later on, when you try to go back for further information, it may have been 'lost', the social workers may have moved on or it would involve you in another trip half-way round the world. For children who were abandoned, including those from overseas, you will clearly have much less to go on.

Do not despair! It is still possible to re-create a meaningful life story for your child. Everyone's life narrative is a construction from personal memories, first-hand accounts and expectations, interspersed with guess work. We all, to a degree, create our stories in retrospect and fill in the blanks. It is the same for your child, only more so: it will probably require far *more* lateral thinking, detective work and imagination on your part. **This can help your child feel she does exist – as long as you start from what you do know, do not intentionally create a false story, and are able to let her know that this is what you believe may have happened to her, rather than absolute fact.**

You will have to suspend judgements, and remain as objective as you can whilst handling this intensely personal issue. Try to think yourself into your child's shoes and imagine what it would be like to be relinquished for adoption, or neglected or intimidated or frightened all the time. Remember that for your child at the time this was her *whole* life, all she knew. Her responses to it may still be very intense and unaltered by other experiences of life. She needs to hear, *over and over,* that it was not her fault. She needs to know it is O.K. to feel angry, sad or confused *and* still want to be back with her birth family.

Your child will not be able to keep two conflicting sets of feelings within her simultaneously. So whilst she may be aware that she was **hurt** by her family, she may only hold on to the love she needed from them. Her underlying pain and rage may then be directed at you, particularly if you give critical messages about them. Being told that her parents loved her can also conflict with her deepest sense of **abandonment** and **shame**. If they had loved her they wouldn't have 'given her away'. So she may conclude either that she was unlovable and bad, that you stole her away, or a combination of both.

Emphasising the positive points about her birth family may invalidate her infantile feelings of *abandonment* **and terror; emphasising the negative points may diminish her** *self-esteem* **or challenge her previous,** *ambivalent attachments.* It is a question of balance, which you need to tread with great care.

As your child grows you will need to continue to work on her life story book. A loose leaf folder or file can allow you to add more information as you go. Soon, there may be more of her life spent with your family than before she came to you, both chronologically and in terms of content. You can give her some idea of time passing by drawing a time bar, vertically, on the side of each page. Your child can colour in blocks of time to represent how long she stayed in each place. **However, please remember that our sense of time and a small child's are very different**.

The first few days, weeks and months of her life (including the pregnancy) were a lifetime to her, though to us they may shrink into relative insignificance. Not only do these times seem life-long to her, they are the foundations for her making sense of her life. The *feeling states* she knew then may persist within her and influence her present functioning very powerfully, even though she cannot consciously recall them. **Never minimise their power or assume, because your child is older and can begin to understand at a more mature thinking level, that she has let go of these infantile feelings deep within.**

In the earliest years, you can begin by trying to obtain photographs of your child before she came home, or any keepsakes, such as the hospital wrist band she wore or the bit of rag she was left in. These are very tangible items, which can help consolidate your little one's fragile *sense of self.* Did anyone else keep copies of photographs, records, or even foetal scans?

If you travelled abroad to fetch your baby home, did you keep the airline tickets, hotel reservations, or the freebies and hand-outs which sometimes go with both? Any documents, formal or informal, that you may have can be lifelines to your child's past. Make contact with other overseas adopters from the same country, they may be able to help you build up your 'fact file'.

Have you remained in contact with birth family members or previous carers, who may give a more personalised account of your child before you knew her? You could try renewing old acquaintances, when this feels right.

If nothing else, you could visit or write to her hospital, birth-place or previous home(s) and try to obtain photographs or descriptions, however long it is since she came home.

You will have to become something of a social archaeologist, digging for cryptic clues about your child and brushing off the dust and cobwebs and, like any historical detective, you will have to be creative, making inspired connections. **The trail becomes colder and more confused with time, so try not to leave it too long!**

Some children have a tendency to destroy their life-story books or other irreplaceable documents – it is well worth making copies of everything. **Remember too that a child can** easily become overwhelmed with feelings or (non-verbal) memories whilst 'doing life-story work'. Stay aware, play it by ear and don't over-do it. Be ready to help your child feel safe again – perhaps with a cuddle, a drink or a funny story.

Disability

It is impossible to cover every disability in any depth here, but some general issues are discussed below. Your young child may have disabilities in addition to his losses and *hurts* from the past. This can sometimes compound his relationship and developmental difficulties and it often becomes difficult to tease out one from the other. **If your child's disability involved time in hospital or painful medical treatments this may also have affected his ability to trust.** A young child cannot distinguish between painful experiences which are abusive and ones in which the motive is to improve his long-term well-being: such treatments may still be perceived as *traumatic hurts* by powerful adults who should be taking care of him.

If your child currently requires specific medical treatment, you will need to find ways of reducing the additional distress these will cause, by explaining simply and repeatedly what is going to happen and staying with your child through these painful experiences (see also page 29). If he has sensory impairments, such as hearing or visual loss, this can interfere with the *sensori-motor* developmental process directly and again you will need to find additional ways to alleviate his distress, to build up your relationship, to learn to communicate and to compensate for his sensory losses.

Try to make contact with other parents who have a child with a similar disability, through Adoption UK or through specific, national or local organisations. Find out as much as you need about the disability, including predictions for your child's future, **and remember that you can always make a difference.**

In some cases, a disability can be an advantage to you and your child in terms of your relationship. If your youngster needs your help for a longer period, this can make it more acceptable for you to encourage dependence and physical closeness. As with any child, your ultimate goal will be independence, as far as it is possible, but the dependence 'piece' of the process has to come first.

Having to lift and move your child physically, or guide him in his own movements, can give you both extra chances for closeness. Physiotherapy exercises can offer the same kinds of opportunities: seize them while you can!

Using signing systems, (such as British Sign Language or Makaton) as an adjunct to hearing and speech, can also put you in touch and allows you to mould your child's hand gently into the word shape, in a way that you cannot with spoken words. Why not try this anyway with your child, whether you feel that communication is problematic or not? In their book *Baby Signs*, Acredolo and Goodwyn (see the Reading List at back of book) argue powerfully that even very young children may communicate through mutually agreed signs, well before they begin to use spoken words.

Sometimes, too, a child with a disability has *alternative abilities*: a heightened awareness of one or more body senses or an innocence which allows him to reach out and touch other people's hearts. This must be nature's way of giving such a child a special gift to help him survive in this world.

The Spiritual Dimension

Healing can take place on many levels – from the physical, to the emotional, to the psychological, to the intellectual, to the spiritual. Wherever possible, elements of each have been included, and interwoven, throughout this book. In the Western, scientific tradition, we often dismiss the intimate connection between *psyche* (mind) and *soma* (body) and overlook the spiritual dimension entirely. Eastern traditions may have something to teach us about the unity of body–mind and about the healing power of spirituality.

Whether we think of the spiritual in terms of orthodox religion, the personal uniqueness within, the community of human beings, or the energies of the natural world, we should not lose touch with its powers. In a sense our children have received insults on every level and, perhaps most of all, at that intangible, spiritual level.

Try to provide your child with additional experiences of spiritual awareness which suit your personal beliefs.

For some, the community and fellowship of the church, synagogue, mosque, temple or secular group may be a powerful source of support and inspiration. You could introduce your young child to these, at first through your personal experiences and then more directly, as she matures.

For others, the wonders of the earth and of nature are life-affirming and empowering. Your little one, too, can benefit from becoming aware of, and feeling, the energies of trees, flowers, mountains, streams, rocks, seas, wind, rain, sunshine, for example. You can use his developing senses to touch, see, feel, hear, smell and move amongst the myriad splendours of the creation, however you may understand it.

Human creativity can also put us in touch with the spiritual dimension. Music, fine arts, expressive media like dance and drama, and acts of great humanity and love within our human community can all touch our hearts and lift our spirits.

Although your child may be initially unresponsive to even the most tangible world, he also has within him the capacity, like all small children and animals, to touch the intangible. It is usually only with age that we come to value the logical over the creative and intuitive, so that in some ways even our very *hurt* children have something on their side.

Moving On

Some of you, perhaps with young children who have been very deeply *hurt*, will wish to join parents of older adopted children in reading *Next Steps in Parenting the Child Who Hurts: Tykes and Teens*. This companion volume offers further suggestions for managing children who *hurt*. However, one of the principal intentions of *First Steps* has been to avoid many of the serious challenges such children may face, by beginning gently, and early on, to heal their lives. Only when we have tried every available strategy in our 'usual' repertoire may we need to go beyond the realms of the usual to reach out to children whose experiences have been so far from usual that they have no awareness of 'normality' upon which to base their lives. It is up to us to establish a new normality for our children, which in time may become internalised as part of their 'normal' behaviours. *Next Steps* was first published in 1999.

Closing Thoughts

I hope that you will feel encouraged and inspired on your first steps with your child by the philosophy, principles and suggestions in this book. They are just the beginning. I believe that every one of you can be creative and draw out of them what you need for *your* child, the one that only *you* know best. I trust that you will take what you need now, and perhaps come back for more, as and when you need. I will always be pleased to hear from you, with comments or questions – although I cannot promise to have all of the answers!

I wish you good luck on these first steps of your journey with your child. It may take you your whole life-time but each day will bring you fresh opportunities to connect with every dimension of this vibrant, fascinating world and to continue making that vital difference to your child's life.

Glossary

A

abandoned

children who are 'given up' for adoption may experience this as being abandoned. Similarly, infants who are left for long or repeated periods may feel as if they have been abandoned

adaptive

helping to keep us alive, on an evolutionary or personal level

ADD/ADHD

these are common medical terms for a cluster of symptoms, including poor attention and impulsive and often hyperactive behaviours

alternative abilities

this gives us a different way of thinking about 'dis'abilities. Individuals may show compensating sensitivities or skills in other areas

arousal

the body and mind's responses to everything which goes on inside and out. Vital within normal 'comfort' limits. Unhelpful when there is too little or too much

associated

connected, integrated on many levels

associations

> these are the connections between senses, behaviours, feelings, awareness, memory processes and areas of the brain and nervous systems which are established throughout life

attachment

> a persisting relationship between two individuals. For a child the attachment relationship initially involves complete dependency and facilitates survival at the biological level

secure attachment

> a healthy pattern of relating, balancing dependence and independence needs

insecure attachment

> insecure attachment patterns are often described as:

ambivalent

> where the child alternates between clinginess (to keep the adult present), and ignoring (see below) or angry behaviours toward the parent (anger, too, is part of the child's behaviour pattern to increase parental closeness and caregiving behaviours)

anxious

> where the child tends to be excessively clingy in an attempt to improve her sense of security and increase caregiving interactions with the parent

avoidant

> where the child seeks to reduce her distress by appearing not to care or to need the parent (since previous parent figures have been unreliable or hurtful)

unattached

> very rarely a child may experience such total deprivation, isolation or maltreatment that s/he does not appear to develop any pattern of attachment

autistic spectrum disorder

> a range of behaviours which present features consistent with autism, to a greater or lesser degree. Typified by a limited ability to form and use social relationships

autonomic nervous system

> the part of the nervous system responsible for involuntary responses. Includes a network of glands and hormones mediating experience and behaviour

avoiding

> tending to be fearful of close contact and relationships, stemming from early, hurtful experiences

B

basic trust

> the level of trust an infant develops in her caregiver(s), and hence the world, through repeated gratification of the 'need cycle'

bio-chemistry

> the functions and interactions of the chemistry of the body

body rhythm
> the natural body patterns, including waking and sleeping

boundaries
> the personal limits by which an individual can define herself, experience herself as separate from others and having personal agency

brain stem
> developmentally the 'oldest' part of the brain, which regulates our breathing and heart rates (and basically defines whether we are alive or not)

C

child, inner
> a way of referring to states of inner feeling formed in childhood which can continue to influence beliefs, thinking and behaviours (from Penny Parks)

child, inside
> see above. Often used in dissociative disorders field, e.g. by Colin Ross. May appear subjectively to an individual as if existing separately. Behaviour may reflect this 'as if' quality

child within
> see above. Used as title of book by Catherine Munroe

cognitive
> conscious thinking processes, in the cerebral cortex of the brain

compliant
> tending to please others. Can be problematic in the extreme, since it places others before self and denies the person's own needs

constricted
> restricted, reduced field of interest, experience or function

container
> one who provides security/safety for attachment and exploration – either physically or emotionally

contain/ing
> providing security and boundaries – either physically or psychologically

containment
> provision of security, either emotional or physical, usually by parent or other trusted adult

cortical neurological system
> the nervous system within the cortex, the most human 'thinking' brain

critical formative periods
> periods of maximum growth and development in childhood, during which relatively small adversities may pose serious challenges to development

D

deep pressure
firm pressure exerted deep into the tissues of the body, in contrast with superficial contact with skin areas

development
the process of moving from the total dependence of a new-born towards the (relative) independence of adulthood. It implies growth and change at physical, emotional, psychological, intellectual and spiritual levels

developmental
the process of growing and maturing through which every child passes, albeit at a unique pace and in her own way. 'Normal' developmental progress implies functional age which matches actual, chronological age

dissociated
lacking or losing connection or meaning. Out of touch with some area of normal awareness

dissociation
loss of connections between senses, feelings, knowledge, behaviours, memories or areas of the nervous system, leading to a weakened ability to make sense of self or others, or to learn from new experience

dissociative response
an adaptive, protective response to being overwhelmed by the amount or content of incoming information. Becomes unhelpful if used too much or continues when things change for the better

diurnal rhythmicity
rhythm of day and night/wakefulness and rest

dyspraxia
often described as 'clumsiness', it is a difficulty of co-ordination, involving the planning, and carrying out, of movement tasks, both small and large

dyspraxic
having difficulties with co-ordination and carrying out of movements

E

empathy
sharing/getting in tune with another's feelings, thoughts, needs

explicit
verbal memory processes, which are usually able to be told

expressive therapy

as opposed to analytical or 'talk' therapies, this kind of therapy encourages expression in many dimensions and may therefore access feelings and memories not readily available to the child verbally

F

feeling states

compartmentalised ways of feeling set in an individual's experience

fight or flight

an early survival mechanism in event of apparent threat – either to stand ground and defend or run away

flashbacks

intense, anxiety producing images from the past which can intrude without warning into present awareness. Can be visual, auditory, smell or body-based

functional

'workable' – offering some kind of advantage to staying alive

G

gaze avert

the tendency to look away when close to another person, which reduces perceived threat (in both directions). Also part of the shame response

good enough

a parent does NOT need to (cannot) be perfect. As long as we get it 'right enough' the child will thrive

gratification

experience of pleasure, relief, satisfaction, comfort

H

hold/ing

containing, providing security and comfort for a baby or small child – can be physical or emotional

holding for nurture

time set aside to provide comfort, security and improved opportunities for closeness and communication through physical holding

holding therapy

an expressive therapy which employs physical holding by a trained psychotherapist to bring about effective healing

holding time

first used by Martha Welch, to describe time deliberately and regularly set aside, for the child with the parent. It involves physically holding the child in close, face-to-face, and allowing free expression of feelings in order to increase closeness in the relationship

homoeostatic/stasis

the maintenance of 'normal' balance or function in our body functions

hurt (also hurting/ful)

Greg Keck and Regina Kupecky used the term 'hurt' in the title of their book *Adopting The Hurt Child* (see Reading List at back of book). It implies the 'wounding' and pain which traumatised children still carry with them from their earliest times. It also, in the context of this book, implies their potential to hurt others as a result of their inner pain

hyperactive

extremely 'busy', over-active, 'on the go', non-stop

hyperkinesis

also known as hyperactivity, especially physical activity

hyper-sensitive

greater sensitivity and responses to experience than 'normally' expected. Often sensitised by earlier trauma, including in the womb and at birth

hyper-vigilant

unable to relax watchfulness for fear-producing events or stimuli, due to continuing internal arousal

hypo-sensitive

less than 'normally expected' ability to respond to sensory or motor stimuli

I

implicit (memory)

memory without words. Can be non-verbal or pre-verbal or automatic memory

impulsivity

tendency to react without thinking of consequences

inner working model

the internal 'maps' which an individual builds up about the world and about herself from her experiences (Bowlby). Once established they tend to be fairly resistant to change, since subsequent perceptions are 'selected' to fit what is expected

integrated

brought into the system and made part of a coherent whole

K

kindle/ing

 tendency to over-respond to even minor or pleasant experiences, leading to exaggerated (fear) responses

L

limbic system

 An important part of the mid-brain (or animal brain) which controls, amongst other things, emotion, motivation and memory functions

M

mid brain

 younger than the brain stem in evolutionary terms and responsible for functions such as body rhythms, emotion, motivation, sexuality and fight, or flight and freeze

mirror/ing

 responding and reflecting back to the child aspects of her expressions, movements, feelings

model

 to demonstrate through example. An infant learns initially through observing and responding to parental models

modulate

 to bring into (reasonable) balance, regulate

modulate neuro-physiological arousal

 the ability to lower and raise levels of response in the nervous system, within comfortable limits

modulation of arousal

 the ability to moderate reaction to internal and external information within comfortable limits

mothering figure

 this is the single most important person in a very young child's life. In our society it is still usually the mother. Whatever the gender, this is the person who provides the mothering which is essential to an infant's survival and well-being

N

neuro-hormones

 the internal bio-chemical secretions which enable transmission of information within the brain and nervous system

neurological connections

 the links between individual nerve cells and specific areas of the brain/nervous system which need to be laid down and reinforced through repeated use

neurological organisation

developmental organising of connections within the nervous systems

neurological system

made up of central nervous system and autonomic nervous system and including the structures of the brain

neuro-physiological

relating to the biology of the brain and nervous systems

neuro-physiologist

a scientist who studies the biology and functioning of the brain and nervous systems

neuro-physiology

the study of the functioning of the brain and nervous systems

night terrors

flashback-like intrusions within sleep, producing intense fear even though the individual is not fully awake

O

object constancy

establishment of an internal way of thinking which allows an individual to know something exists when it is not actually visible, tangible, audible, etc.

olfactory bulbs

primary smell receptors in direct touch with the limbic system

oral sensitivity

specific sensitivity within the mouth or around the lip and cheek area

over-compliant

an exaggerated willingness to please, at the expense of personal needs. Often derives from inner feelings of self-worthlessness or badness

P

paediatrician

a medical consultant who specialises in the health of children

part

it can help to think of a child as made up of parts relating to different feelings

physical prompts

reminders given to a child through touch/movement

physiological

relating to the biology of the body – how it keeps us alive and responds internally to what is going on around us

post-traumatic stress reaction

a complex pattern of physiological and psychological/emotional responses to overwhelming or chronic stress(es)

praxis

carrying out of movement tasks

predisposition

tendency towards particular characteristics or traits, carried in the genes, which may or may not be expressed in the individual

primary caregiver

the child's main source of physical and emotional security, the main attachment figure (see mother figure)

prone

horizontal, face down body position

proprioception

awareness of one's physical body, its sensations and movement capabilities

psyche

the mind, soul or spirit

psychic

of the mind, soul or spirit (often used in contrast to the body, or soma)

psychological containment

Winnicott proposed that for a young child to develop a sense of security, she needs to experience being emotionally held by the parenting figure. In that way she also learns to manage her own feelings and emotions

psychological representation

structure or framework to 'map' internal patterns of belief, thought, behaviour

psychological trauma

the (long-term) effects on behaviour, feeling and thinking of overwhelming experiences

R

rage cycle

also known as the needs cycle, this model illustrates the stages of distress, arousal and satisfaction through which an infant moves, over and over again each day

referent looking

infants derive a sense of security and a sense of themselves as individuals by regularly referring back to the mother's facial and body expressions. Toddlers also look back at a familiar figure to gain reassurance and confidence as they move away and explore the unfamiliar

reflecting back

acting as a mirror to another's actions/feelings

regress/ion

going back to 'earlier' developmental patterns of behaviour. Often occurs under stress. Can be therapeutic if it allows completion of unfinished developmental tasks and occurrence of new learning

regulation

the ability to monitor and maintain, within comfortable limits, feelings, emotions, body functions and responses

reinforce

to make more likely to happen again, to accentuate

re-kindle

to set off an exaggerated pattern of reactions, not appropriate to the actual situation

resolution

reaching a stage of relative calm (after an emotional storm). Usually involves gaining greater understanding, insight or self-control

S

safe holding

elective holding to provide additional nurturing, security, comfort and opportunities for closeness and communication

selective attention

ability to pick out important, striking or frightening aspects of the surroundings and focus on them to the exclusion of less important information

self

who we are, our awareness of self, is derived from the experiences we have. Hence our sense of self may be fluid and responsive to present as well as past happenings. However, early experience seems to carry the most weight and profoundly to influence future perceptions and interpretations.

Some aspects of self definition are listed below. They all contribute to our knowledge of, and acceptance of who we are and how we react, in response to our self (self-reference, our sense of self) and to others:

    self-aware/ness
    self-care
    self-competence
    self-confidence
    self-consciousness
    self-constancy
    self-control
    self-destructive
    self-esteem
    self-expression

self-harm/ing
self-identity
self-possessed
self-regulatory/ion
self-respect
self-soothing
self-stimulation

sense of self

see above; derived in major part from reciprocal and mirroring experiences within the attachment relationship

sensori-motor

perceptions and responses of the senses and/or of movement

sensory

relating to the senses

sensory soothing

calming activities which relax any or all of the senses

separation anxiety

an infant is said to show this when she is distressed when separated from the familiar attachment figure

shame

feeling bad about who we are – as opposed to guilt, feeling bad about what we have done. In small doses it can bring about healthy change, in excess it becomes toxic, affecting our sense of self-respect, self-worth, self-esteem

soma

relating to the body

soothing

calming and comforting from inside or from outside

spatial awareness

the sense of one's body position in space

stimulation

raising of levels of arousal or functioning

stimuli

incoming information of every sort which can influence perception and responses on an internal or external level

stochastic

discrete patches of experience, experienced as on/off, for example black/white, present/absent

stranger anxiety

>   babies of around six or seven months old are said to show increased distress in the presence of unfamiliar figures. They tend to turn to the mothering figure, or other familiar person, for reassurance

switched off

>   shutting down of feelings, responses, interactions in an attempt to avoid further fear or pain. A dissociative technique often used by avoidant children

switching off

>   a child who feels threatened or afraid or ashamed may respond by distancing herself emotionally from her surroundings temporarily, through dissociating. This can become habitual and can prevent the child learning about the comfort and security of closeness

switching out

>   see above. Tendency to move awareness away from current environment, often going 'inside', into another part of self, as a protective response to a perceived threat

synchronic attunement

>   the harmonising effect seen between parent and infant, which has been shown to enable an infant to alter her body rhythms and internal responses to match the parent's and hence learn to regulate her own. Hence to 'get in sync with'

T

tactile sensory defensiveness

>   under- or over-reactivity to touch. Contact is often experienced as painful or frightening

time out

>   short periods of time spent quietly (and usually alone) – allows time to think/calm down

transitional object

>   Usually a tangible 'something' representing the security and comfort of the mother figure, which is available to the infant at times of brief separation

trauma

>   literally, a wound. Normally taken to mean an overwhelming experience, which does not allow the individual to return to a 'normal', comfortable state of being. There are demonstrable biological and bio-chemical changes associated with feelings of powerlessness, lack of control, panic or numbing

traumatic

>   adjective used to describe experiences and responses to trauma

trigger

>   according to trauma theory, once a pattern of behaviour has come into being, a much smaller stimulus may set off the same level of response, over and over again

V

vestibular stimulation

stimulation of the balance structures within the middle ear, brain and nervous systems; necessary for developing sense of balance and body position

W

withdrawal

going into oneself, disconnecting (dissociating) from people/surroundings. Once protective, but can interfere with ability to relate

Reading List

Acredolo, L. and Goodwyn, S. (1996) *Baby Signs*. London: Hodder and Stoughton.

Ayres, A. Jean (1994) *Sensory Integration and the Child*. WPS.

Black, Dora, Newman, Martin, Harris-Hendriks, Jean and Mezey, Gillian (1997) *Psychological Trauma*. London: Gaskell.

Bowlby, John (1988) *A Secure Base*. London: Routledge.

Brazelton, Terry and Cramer, Bertrand, G. (1991) *The Earliest Relationship*. London: Karnac Books.

Brière, John (1992) *Child Abuse Trauma*. London: Sage.

Chennells, Prue and Morrison, Marjorie (1995) *Talking About Adoption*. London: British Agencies for Adoption and Fostering.

Delaney, Richard (1991) Fostering Changes. Fort Collins: WJC.

Delaney, Richard and Kunstal, Frank (1993) *Troubled Transplants*. National Child Welfare Resource Center for Management and Administration, University of Southern Maine.

Fahlberg, Vera (1994) *A Child's Journey Through Placement*. London: British Agencies for Adoption and Fostering.

Field, Tiffany and Reite, Martin (1985) *The Psychobiology of Attachment and Separation*. New York, NY: New York Academic Press.

Freeman, Lorey and Deach, Carol (1986) *Loving Touches*. Seattle, WA: Parenting Press Inc.

Freeman, Lorey and Deach, Carol (1993) *It's My Body*. Seattle, WA: Parenting Press Inc.

Gil, Eliana and Bodmer-Turner, Jeffrey (1994) *Someone in My Family Has Molested Children*. Rockville, MD: Launch Press.

Green, Christopher (1995) *Understanding Attention Deficit Disorder*. London: Vermilion.

Greenberg, Mark, Cicchetti, Dante and Cummings, E. Mark (1990) *Attachment in the Preschool Years*. Chicago: University of Chicago Press.

van Gulden, Holly and Bartels-Rabb, Lisa (1993) *Real Parents, Real Children*. New York, NY: Crossroad.

Herman, L. Judith (1992) *Trauma and Recovery*. London: Pandora.

Howe, David (1996a) *Adopters on Adoption*. London: British Agencies for Adoption and Fostering.

Howe, David (1996b) *Attachment Theory for Social Work Practice*. London: British Agencies for Adoption and Fostering.

James, Beverly (1989) *Treating Traumatized Children*. London: Lexington Books.

James, Beverly (1995) *Handbook for the Treatment of Attachment Trauma Problems in Children*. Lexington, MA: Lexington Books.

Keck, Gregory and Kupecky, Regina (1995) *Adopting The Hurt Child*. CO: Pinon Press.

Kehoe, Patricia and Deach, Carol (1987) *Something Happened and I'm Scared to Tell*. USA: Parenting Press Inc.

Klein, Josephine (1995) *Our Need For Others*. London: Routledge.

van der Kolk, B. McFarlane, A. and Weisaeth, L. (1996) *Traumatic Stress*. New York, NY: Guilford.

Kupecky, Regina (1996) *Romanian Life Story Book*. Cleveland, OH: Desk Top Publishing..

McIntee, Jeanie (1992) *Trauma, The Psychological Process*. Chester, Cheshire: Desk Top Publishing.

McNamara, Joan (1995) *Bruised Before Birth*. London: British Agencies for Adoption and Fostering.

Montagu, Ashley (1986) *Touching – The Human Significance of Skin*. New York, NY: Perennial.

Munroe, Catherine (1993) *The Child Within*. London: Children's Society.

Perry, Bruce (1993) 'Trauma I and II' in 'The Advisor'. *American Professional Society on the Abuse of Children 6*, Spring, 14–18, Summer, 1 14–19.

Peterson, Janelle (1994) *The Invisible Road*. DTP (US).

Pinto, G. and Feldman, M. (1996) *Homoeopathy for Children*. Wellingborough, Northamptonshire: Thorsons.

Pithers, Gray, Cunningham and Lane (1993) *From Trauma to Understanding*. Brandon, VT: Safer Society Press.

Randolph, Elizabeth (1994) *Children Who Shock and Surprise*. Evergreen, CO: RFR.

Ross, Colin A. (1997) *Dissociative Identity Disorder*. Chichester: Wiley.

Ryan, Tony and Walker, Rodger (1993) *Life Story Work*. London: British Agencies for Adoption and Fostering.

Schore, Allan (1994) *Affect Regulation and the Origin of Self*. Hillsdale, NJ: Lawrence Erlbaum Associates Inc.

Southgate, John (1996) *An Attachment Perspective on Dissociation and Multiplicity*. London: Centre for Attachment-based Psychoanalytic Psychotherapy (CAPP).

Stettbacher, J. Konrad (1992) *Making Sense of Suffering*. London: Meridian.

Sykes, Lenni (1995) *The Natural Hedgehog*. London: Gaia Books Ltd.

Tisserand, Maggie (1990) *Aromatherapy for Women*. London: Thorsons.

Umansky, W. and Steinberg-Smalley, B. (1993) *ADD – Helping Your Child Untie the Knot of Attention Deficit Disorders*. London: Warner Books.

Verny, Tom (1982) *The Secret Life of the Unborn Child*. London: Sphere.

Verri⸱⸱ Nancy (1994) *The Primal Wound*. Baltimore, MD: Gateway.

Waite⸱⸱, Elizabeth A. (1993) *Trauma and Survival*. New York, NY: Norton.

Waites, Elizabeth A. (1997) *Memory Quest*. New York, NY: Norton.

Walker, Peter (1995) *Baby Massage*. London: Piatkus.

Welch, Martha (1988) *Holding Time*. Hemel Hempstead: Simon and Schuster.

Welch, Martha (1994) Presentation to ATTACh Conference in Cleveland, OH.

Worwood, Valerie Ann (1995) *The Fragrant Mind*. New York, NY: Doubleday.

de Zulueta, Felicity (1993) *From Pain to Violence*. London: Whurr.

Index